THE 26 SIGNS OF THE ZOMBIE APOCALYPSE

A DOCUMENTATION OF AN ATTEMPT TO COMMUNICATE WITH THE UNDEAD USING AMERICAN SIGN LANGUAGE.

DEVIN SHEEHY
JESSICA BLUNDELL
TARAH WHITAKER

PORKOPOLIS PRODUCTIONS

© 2012 Porkopolis Productions. All Rights Reserved. Unauthorized publication of this work is strictly prohibited.
All illustrations by Devin Sheehy
Photography by Josh Pfeifer and Devin Sheehy
Additional photography by Billy Alexander

Special thanks: Emily Brandehoff for that extra push to get me moving on this project. Josh Pfeifer for his assistance on the art photography, and Paul Trimble whom without I would not have discovered my ability to paint.

Forward

You know what the funny thing is? I don't know sign language! The real origins of this book lie with a zombie hand tattoo I did a number of years ago. It laid the ground work for my own personal style of drawing zombies that appear in this book. Then one day in 2010 I had an epiphany while driving to work.

Why not do a sign language book using zombie hands?

So I got to work, well sorta. I drew up the first three letters of the alphabet and then put the project on the back burner for another year. After much personal turmoil and strife I was speaking with an artist friend of mine and I mentioned the stalled project.

She thought it was a great idea and wondered why I hadn't proceeded with book.

Yes, why hadn't I?

So I got to work. It's funny how when producing a book even of this size you like to kid yourself that it's almost done. I figured after finishing the paintings in a short two week span I'd have this one on the shelves within a couple months.

Yet new ideas kept hitting me on ways to expand the book into a larger work. First off it needed a story. I am no writer so I began searching for people interested in helping out. Credit for the first half of the story goes to my friend Tara Whitaker with which I collaborated on the initial story.

I still felt it lacked something, I came to the conclusion that what was needed was some technical writing. In Jessica Blundell I found just the writer I needed. She ended up writing all the research notes, telegrams and journal entries.

Now you hold in your hands a project long in the making and I hope you enjoy it as much as I did creating it.

Devin Sheehy
2012

About The Authors

Devin Sheehy is the author of a number of publications including *Damn It, Not Another Sketchbook, Machine Theory 101: A Look at the Modern Electric Tattoo Machine for Mentor and Apprentice* and *Paul Trimble Has a Posse*. Hailing from Cincinnati Ohio, Devin has been tattooing since 1995. He has a degree in Graphic Design from Antonelli College in Cincinnati.

Jessica Blundell was raised in Northern California. Growing up riding horses and caring for animals alongside her mother, she grew to become an animal advocate and a prolific writer. She currently spends most of her time gaming and collaborates her work by writing news and reviews for an online media and gaming websites. When approached about working on a Zombie project she jumped at the chance. You would too if you spent a lot of your spare time shooting zombies in the head.

Tarah Whitaker was born & raised in a small suburb in south-western Ohio, Ms. Whitaker thought it might prove interesting to dabble in various subjects at the University of Cincinnati. The experience inspired her to take up a run-of-the-mill Administrative Assistant position, which she actually enjoys, and which allows plenty of time for extracurricular writing collaborations. Mrs. Whitaker is also very grateful for the opportunity, and had a lot of fun with this project!

American Sign Language

American Sign Language (ASL) is a complete, complex language that employs signs made by moving the hands combined with facial expressions and postures of the body. It is the primary language of many North Americans who are deaf and is one of several communication options used by people who are deaf or hard-of-hearing.[1]

L ittle is known about the origin of the outbreak, apart from the United States government's awareness of the zombie threat – long before Z-Day. Recently discovered documents, unearthed by a local Suicide Squad [1], prove the suspicions of many conspiracy theorists.

On January 27, 2019, this particular Squad set out on an expedition in search of supplies and armaments. This event, in and of itself is relatively unremarkable, if extremely dangerous. Most of our readers are well aware that excursions like this have trailed off in recent years, due to the diminishing availability of salvageable material beyond the safety zones of New Castilian's walls.

Despite these discouraging conditions, the team set off on their expedition with high hopes and low expectations. What they found was surprising and unprecedented.

Deep underground, near what was once Louisville, Kentucky, Suicide Squad leader Randal Kelley discovered a military laboratory. Based on evidence found at the scene, the facility, called Lazarus [2], had been abandoned approximately 25 years before Z-Day.

"We never would have found the facility, had it not

been for the uncontrolled fires that had burnt down the office building above. They hid the lab in plain sight." Kelley recalled the experience, shaking his head in disbelief at the memory of his team's findings.

Regarding the documents, another Squad member, Kyra Schon, said, "It was hard to know how long ago the lab had been abandoned. Everywhere we looked there were charred bones among the wreckage. We came across some filing cabinets in an office area, and that's where we found the remains of the documents. Everything was marked classified."

Dating as far back as the 1970's, the documents show evidence that the government not only possessed the Lazarus virus, but that it was also experimenting on test subjects. These unfortunate souls were gathered from penitentiaries across the United States. Most were death-row and life-sentence inmates, according to reports- individuals no one would miss. The subjects were injected with the virus, with the goal of creating mindless super soldiers. The outcome of these ambitions, which is a reality we are all well aware of: there is no controlling the hungry horde.

While much of the research was destroyed, the work of Dr. Benjamin Huss was preserved enough to clarify some of the tests performed on subjects infected with the virus. Dr. Huss was a world-wide expert in the field of communication psychology. His notes, recovered from the lab, express his resolve to find a process of communicating with the undead. The unorthodox research methods eventually turned to American Sign Language (ASL). Dr. Huss believed communication was possible with ASL, when paired with the use of cybernetic implants. These implants were attached to bulky batteries, fastened to the backs of zombies.

Dr. Huss devised a cue card system designed to teach basic American Sign Language to the undead, with the 26 character alphabet as a starting point. Cadaver hands were used for modeling the alphabet, because he believed the infected might respond better to appendages that resembled their own.

The good doctor's tragic flaw was that he assumed the traditional rules of psychology and neurobiology applied to the undead. Ultimately, and unfortunately for the scientists at the Lazarus facility, the knowledge was discovered too late. The Lazarus virus was responsible for the reanimation of the infected, leaving them with no remaining higher brain function. The virus was in control.

Based on reports at the facility, on September 15th, 1976, after proper protocol was ignored, a number of the undead escaped their cells and overran the facility.

General Karl Hardman, the U.S. government attaché who oversaw the Lazarus facility, ordered the lock down and decontamination of the entire compound. The living and undead alike were exterminated and left to rot. The laboratory was sealed off, with the blissfully unaware American public meandering the streets above the facility, on the streets of Louisville and beyond. It still isn't clear how the Lazarus virus came to infect 80% of the planet's population, but this is something we may never find out.

The following is the cue card system developed by Dr. Huss and fragments of his research found at the site.

1 For anyone unfamiliar with Suicide Squads, these are groups of roaming scavengers who bring supplies and information back from the dead zones. The macabre nature of the moniker stems from the suicidal nature of venturing outside of safety zones.

2 The name "Lazarus" may seem familiar, as it is the same name given to the virus responsible for reanimating dead tissue.

The Undead and Human Sign Language
01 Sep 1975

Abstract:
There does not exist a universally accepted definition of language, or criteria for its use; this is one of the reasons that we have decided to test whether or not the undead can use language. Language consists of various aspects. It may be thought that anything the undead can do is not language; of course, if it is accurate that language defines us as humans, and the undead can learn sign language, then would it be correct to say that deaf people who use sign language are not human? I think not.

Introduction:
Why are we trying to teach language to the undead? This project would shed light not only on the nature of language, cognitive and intellectual capacities, as well as such issues as the uniqueness of human language and thought processes of not only humans, but also the undead. A very different reason for teaching language to the infected is that the research would discover better methods for training them.

A new method of communication is necessary when dealing with the undead because they are composed strictly of reanimated flesh. Depending on the level of decomposition most corpse's vocal cords have rotted away. When it comes to the matter of the freshly infected, it has been documented that complex speech requires a highly complex brain which is no longer available to Zeds.

Materials and Method:
In preparing the test subjects obtained from McNeil Island Federal Penitentiary each candidate is examined by a medical professional and washed. Once medical history is verified each subject is then quarantined and fasted for a period of 48 hours. During this time, members of a specified testing group are allotted only water. (This fasting period was not initially planned but added at a later date)

Immediately following the 48 hour quarantine period the testee is then injected with 2ml Lazarus. It is important to note that is 100 percent communicable and fatal.

It takes no less than 4 hours for the subject to change. Once this process is complete the new Zed is taken to a private holding cell where they will remain for the duration of this project or until destroyed.

Each holding cell is behind bullet proof glass, this is done to add a marginal amount to safety to the procedure of teaching the zombies sign language. No actual contact is made between subject and laboratory staff beyond feeding and the changing of battery packs.

Cadaver hands are used in collaboration with electrical shock treatments and food rewards. Cadaver hands were chosen for their likeness to the body of the test subjects. It is assumed that the Zed will learn faster and more effectively if each sign is given with an appendage that resembles th_____ though it is not yet known if the zo_____ess self-awareness, it is hoped that the familiarity will result in less aggression and a sort of curiosity or comfort followed by a willingness to learn.

staff member spends at least 6 hours a [day] with their designated assignments. This time is spent showing the tested [de]signs made with the cadaver hand followed [wit]h a simple command words projected into [the] cell through a speaker system. The subjects [a]re also taught the alphabet so that more c[omplex] methods of communication can eventually [be] achieved. Every laboratory assistant is given only one or two charges. We want to see if a relationship bui[lt on] trust can help the test subjects learn. We a[lso th]ink that each staff member may discover the best method of teaching their assigned test subject after spending enough time with them. Through repetition, punishment and reward it is believed that we will be able to teach these Zed to follow noncomplex commands and possibly a fully functioning ability to communicate.

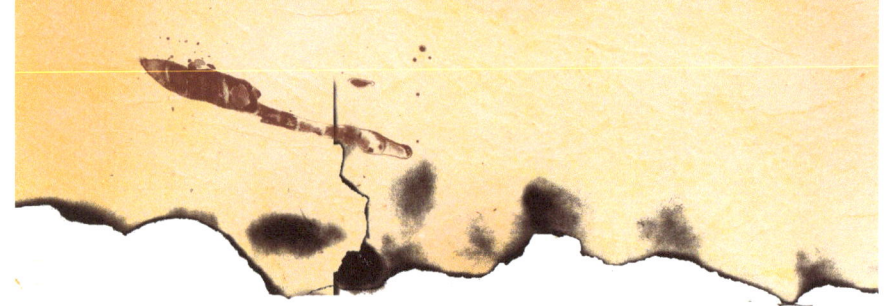

The 26 Signs of the Zombie Apocalypse

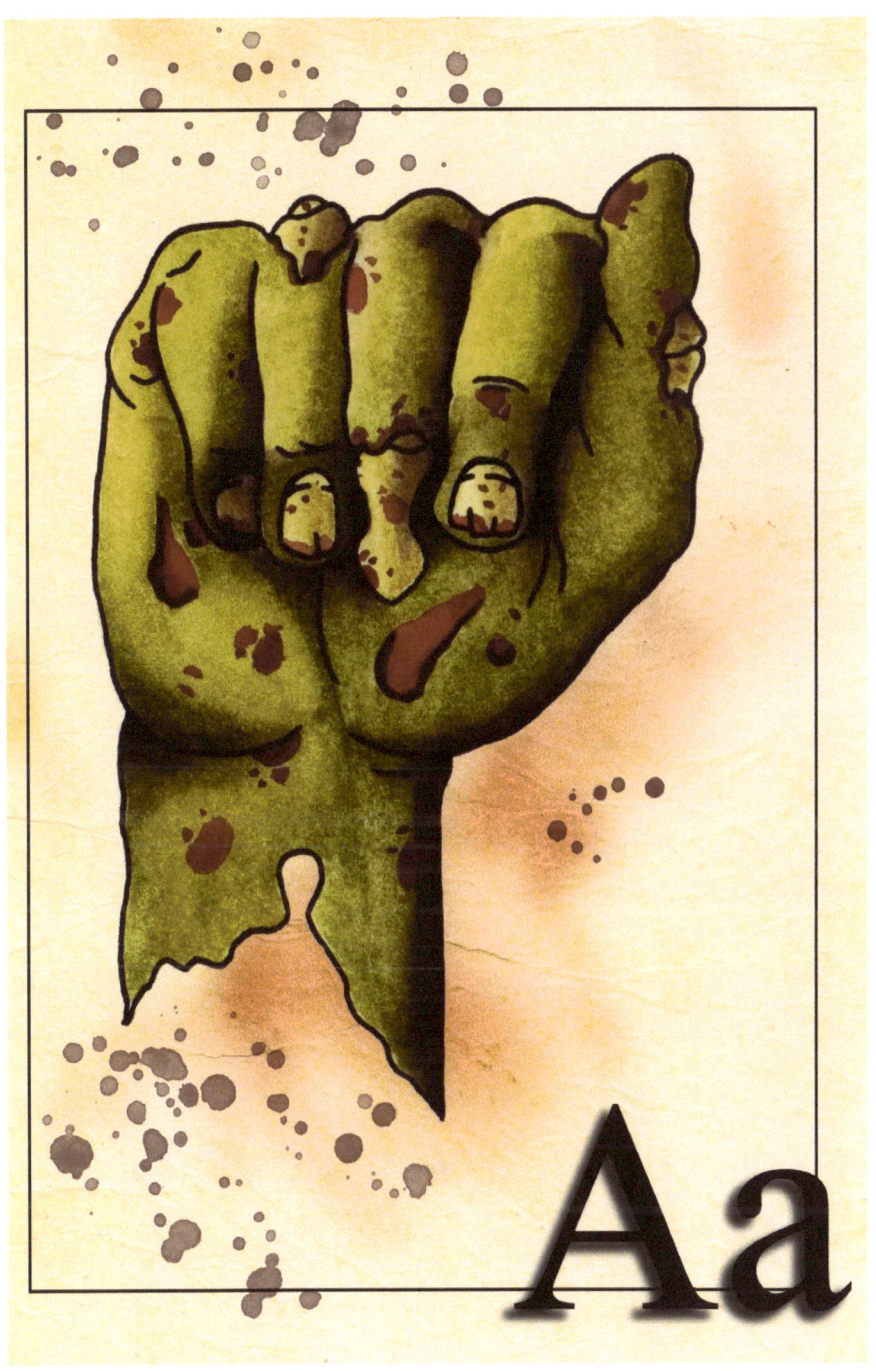

31 Oct 1975,

...ck treatments are not working as i... ...ded. The ZED do not respond as in... ...ded when receiving a small electric ch... ...through the neck. Unlike humans, the ... ...t of pain does not persuade a zom... ...into learning for fear, they instead convulse. I have come to the conclusion that the ZED do not feel pain at all. I had speculated this much from the military documentation I had received at the beginning of my experiments. I had however hoped that the implants would help with this dilemma. Hypothesizing that the implants could not only reactivate dead brainwaves allowing a zombie to learn, I had hoped that they would also allow the zombies to realize that they were being punished. This has not been the case, it seems ability to problem solve ... been recovered.

The 26 Signs of the Zombie Apocalypse

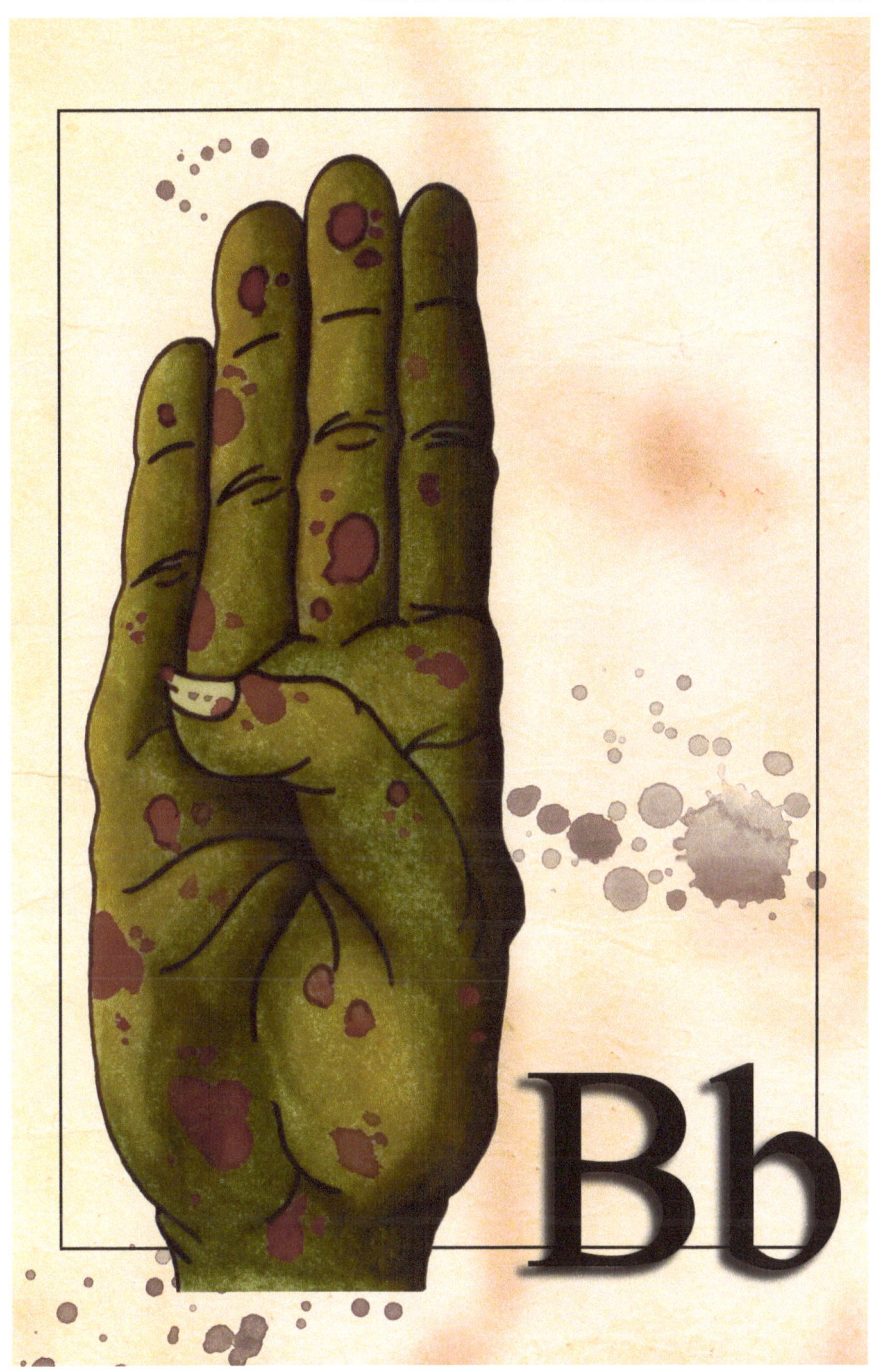

> 07 Dec 1975,
> ...sions have become too much of ... ...ard to endure any longer. I have come to the conclusion that while the zombies do not actually feel the pain, whatever is left of the nervous system still reacts to electricity. Every time a ZED goes into one of these fits our cleaning crew has to clean up all of the bodily fluids, mostly blood and dead tissue that is expelled from the body. Too much time and effort is bei... spent on these hazardous cl... tions. There has to be ... get thes... bi...

We now know the only practical use of electricity against the undead involves cases where the voltage is high enough to completely destroy the brain. This is an exceptionally good tactic when you have a crowd of zombies standing in water. Every Suicide Squad member carries a modified cattle prod for this express purpose.

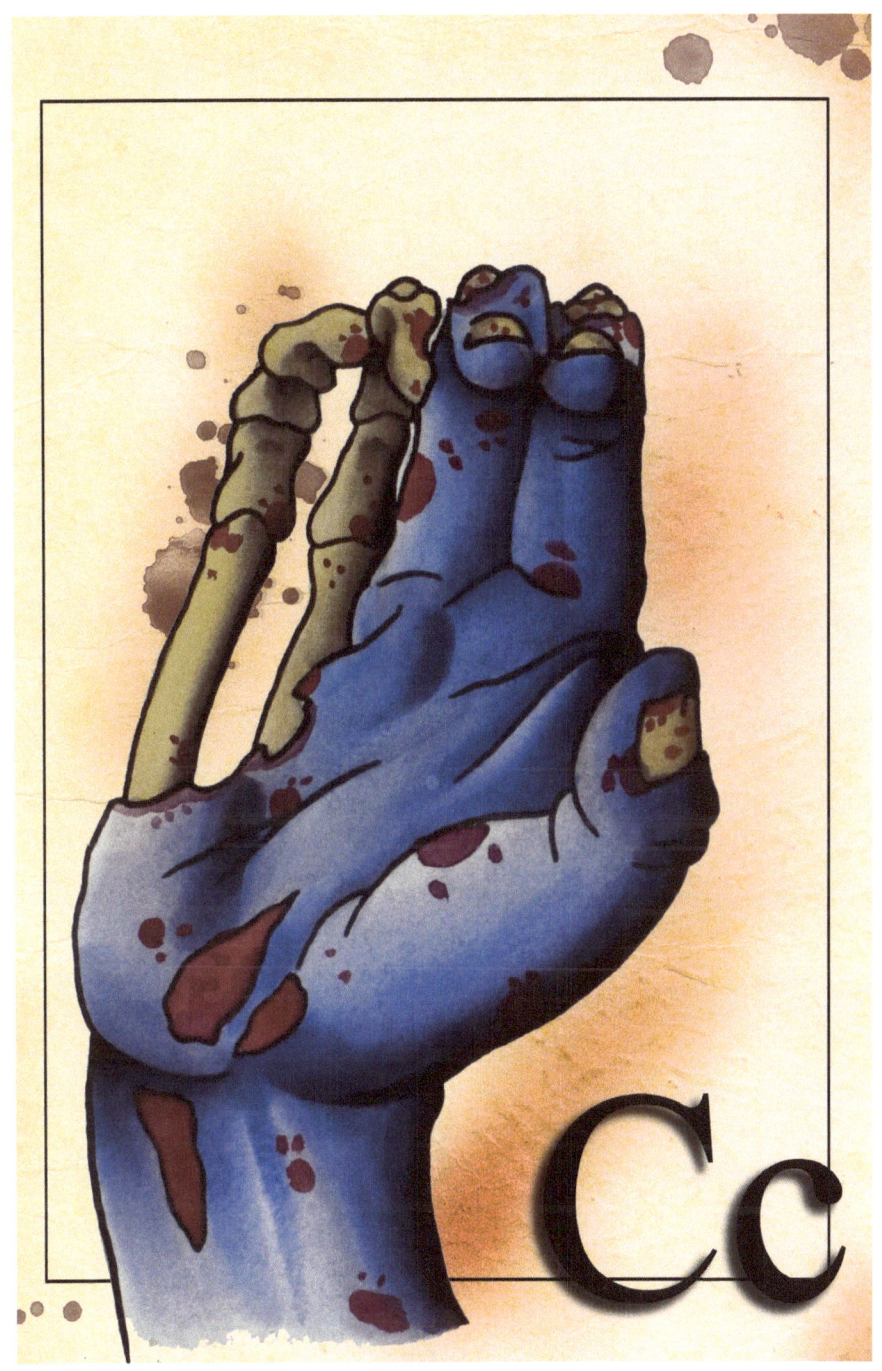

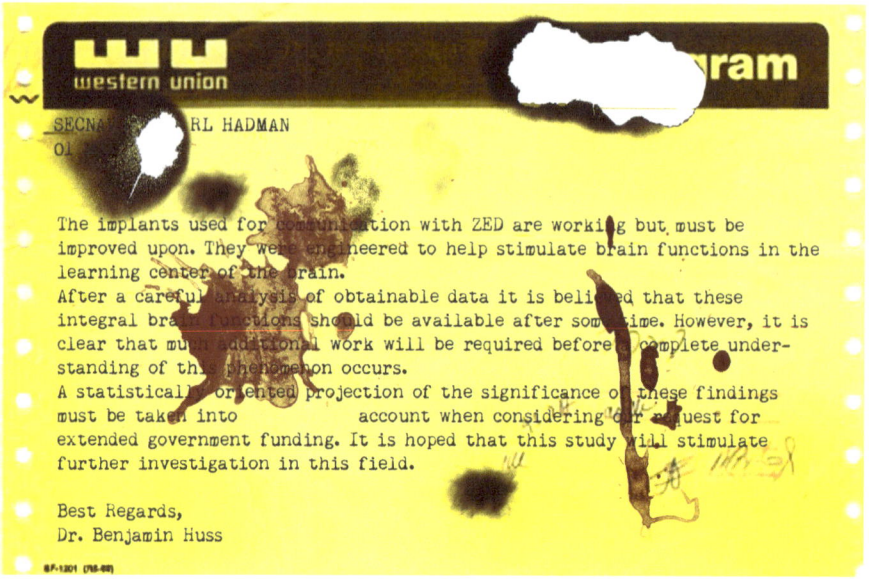

If only Dr. Huss had realized sooner that heightened brain waves in the zombies learning cortex would do nothing at all. When Suicide Squad 1 entered the aforementioned facility they found more than just destruction from the remnants of this documentation. They also found journal entries and writing on the walls. The messages left on the walls of the lab suggest a certain level of insanity, but the message is clear and concise. "The virus is alive" was found over and over again. While this realization might only have been made after it was too late and the facility was in lock down, the message is still true. Since Z-Day, we have come to realize that the lazarus virus does indeed act as a living entity. The undead are walking corpses and nothing more. The reanimation stems solely from the virus. It is alive and in control.

The 26 Signs of the Zombie Apocalypse

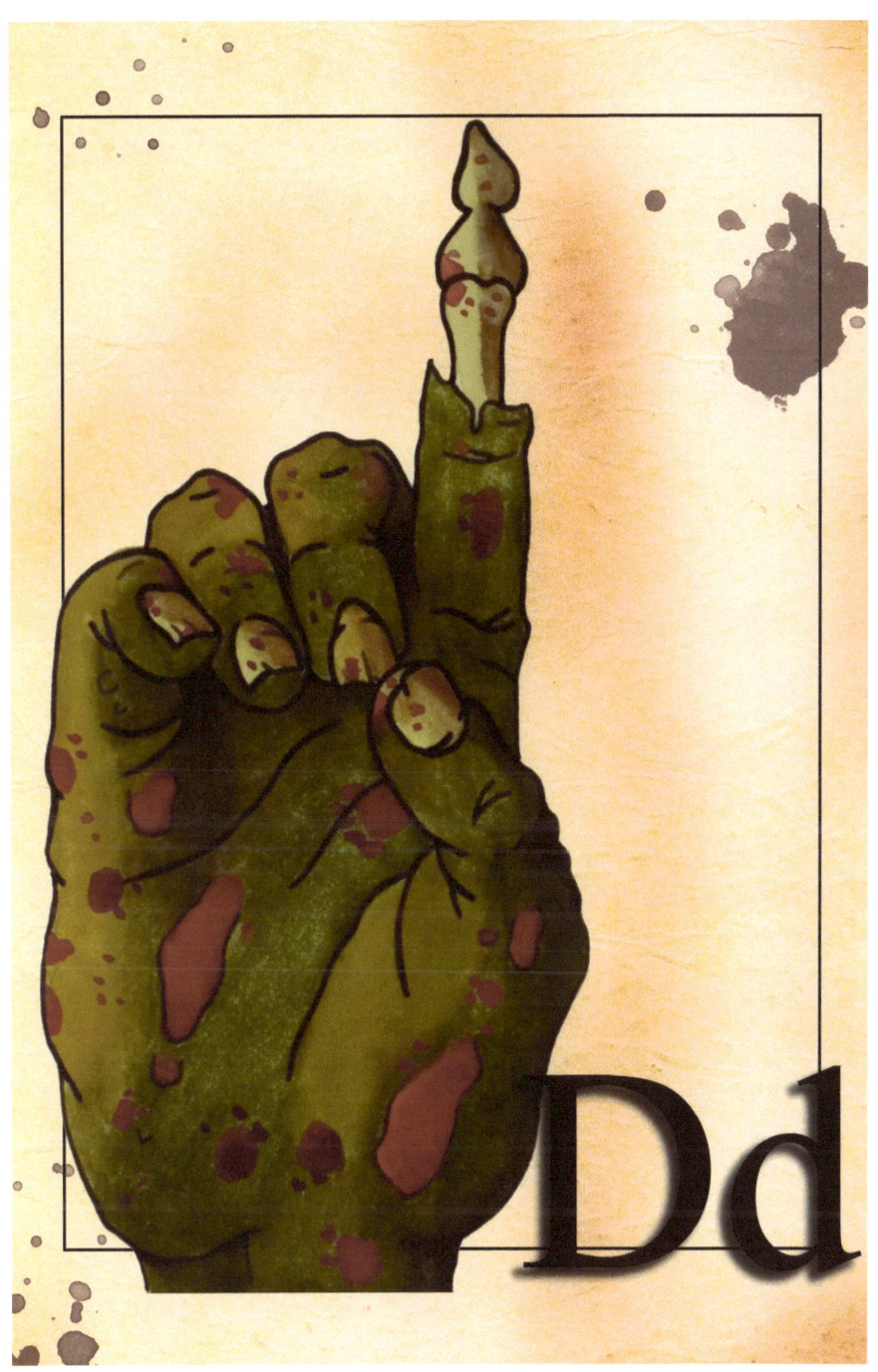

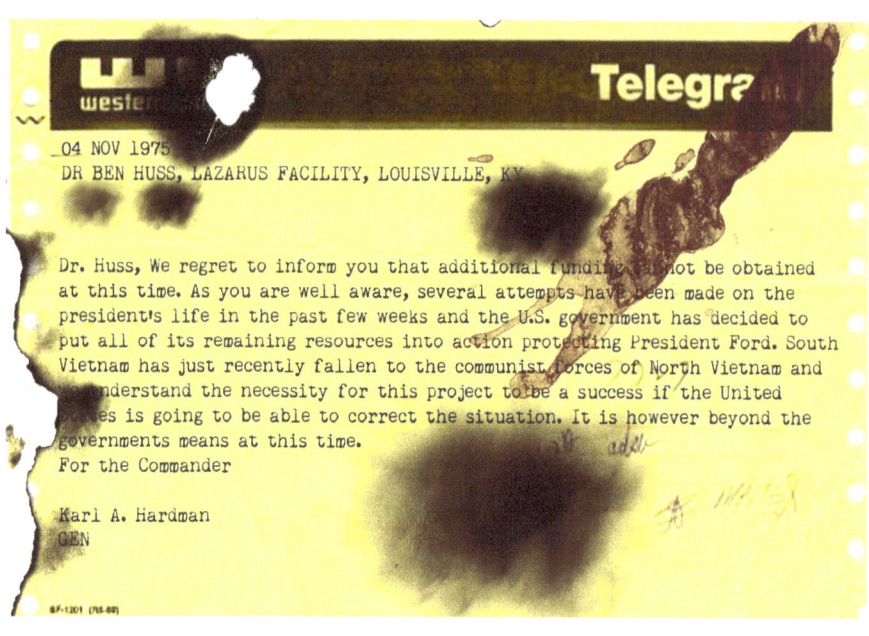

While we no longer have a corrupt government to worry about it is still a sickening thought. Keep in mind that this telegram went out only two months after the beginning of this project. Not only was the U.S. administration spending the people's tax dollars on wars that kill tens of thousands of people, they were also spending a large sum of money on spreading a virus that killed over eighty percent of the world's population. They may have even been the ones responsible for the virus' development.

The 26 Signs of the Zombie Apocalypse

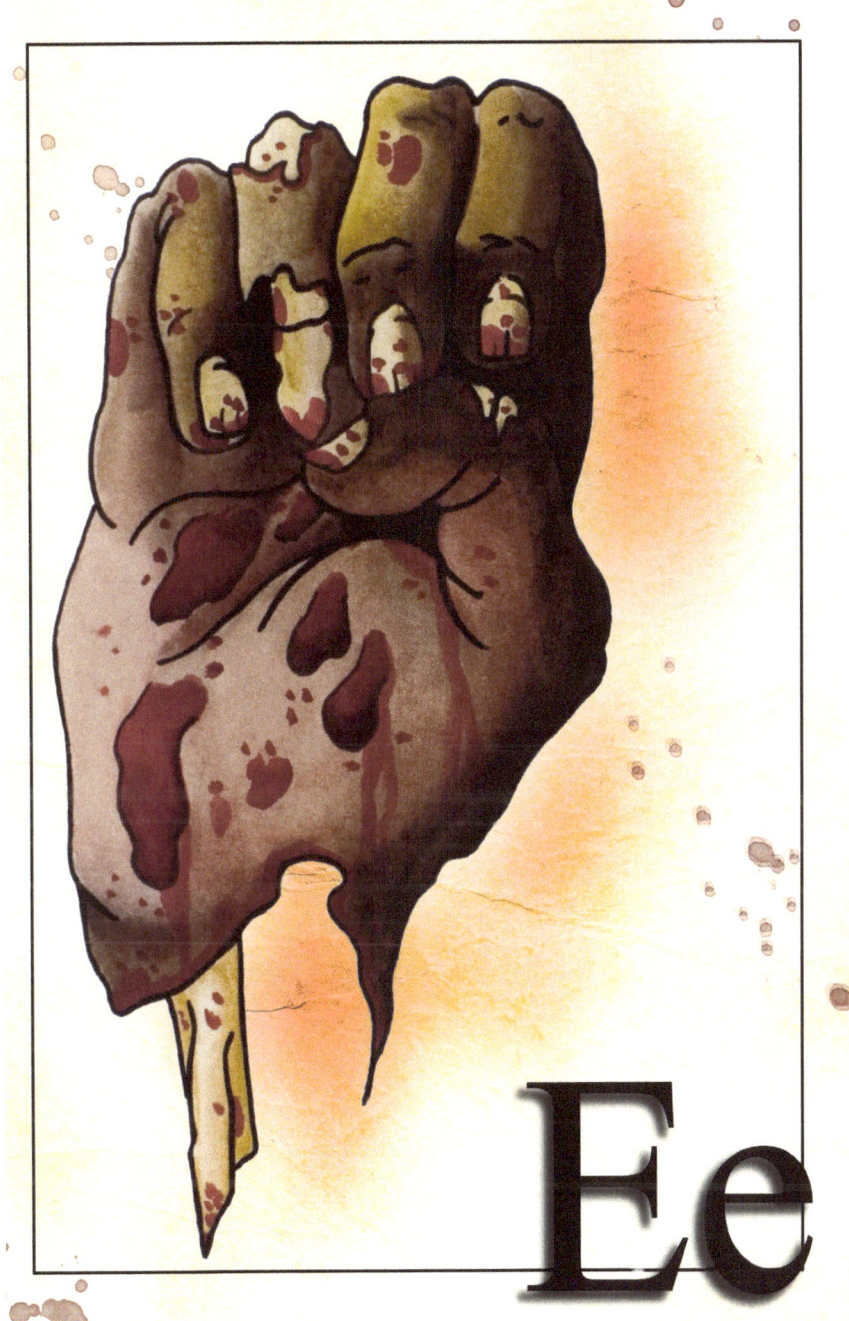

Ee

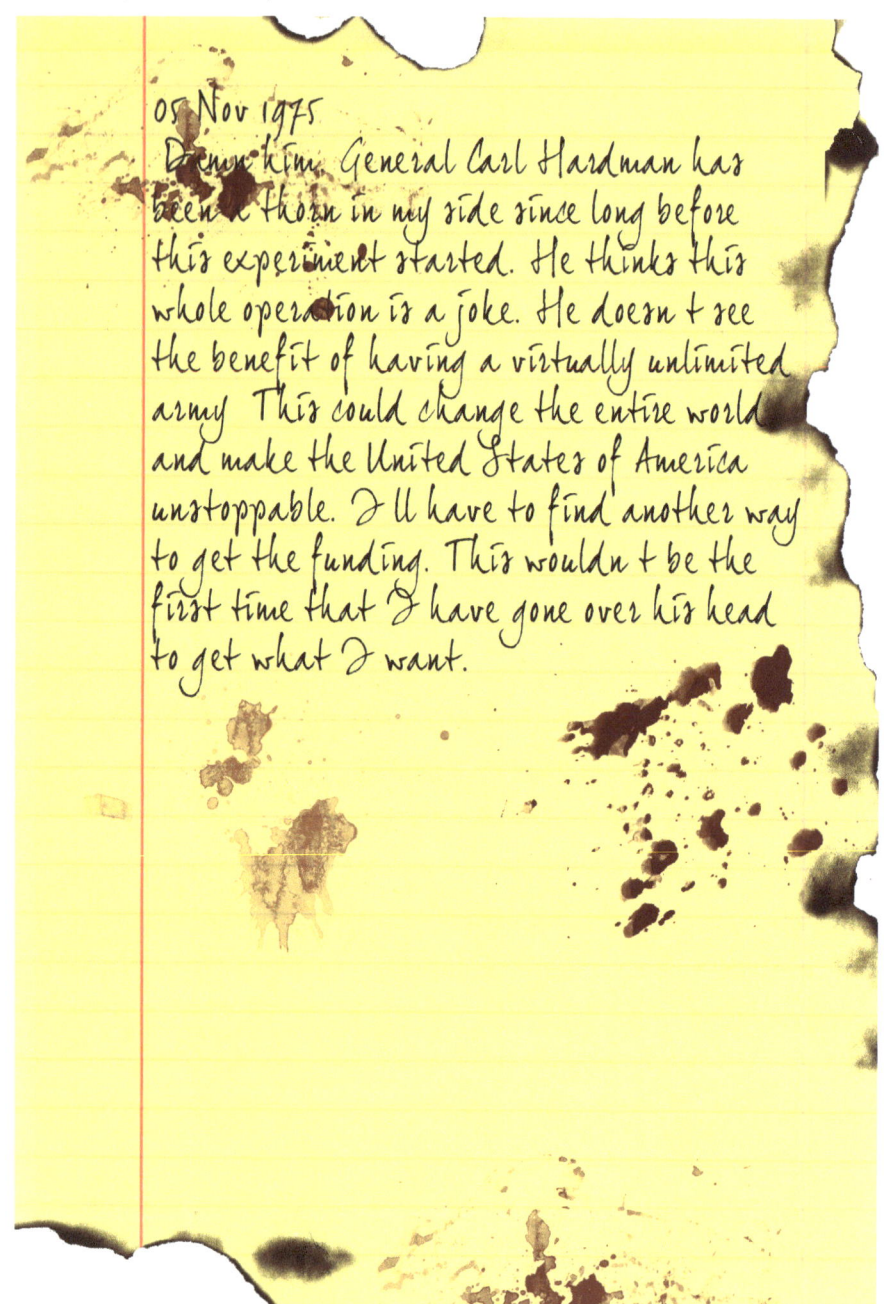

05 Nov 1975

Dear Kim, General Carl Hardman has been a thorn in my side since long before this experiment started. He thinks this whole operation is a joke. He doesn't see the benefit of having a virtually unlimited army. This could change the entire world and make the United States of America unstoppable. I'll have to find another way to get the funding. This wouldn't be the first time that I have gone over his head to get what I want.

The 26 Signs of the Zombie Apocalypse

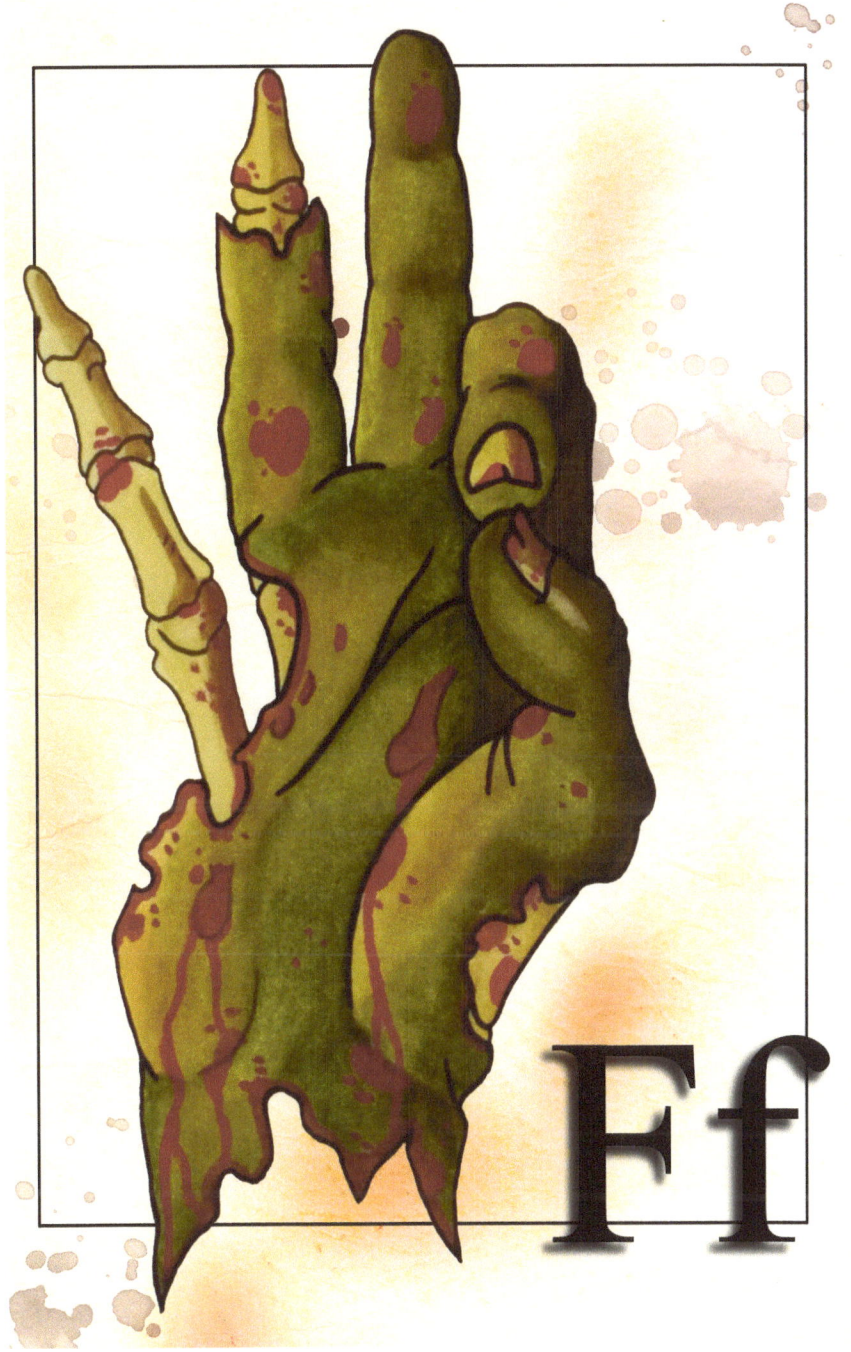

02 Feb 1976,

The need to feed, or the hunger as we have come to call it, seems to heighten in intensity over time. It is getting more and more dangerous to interact directly with each ZED. After only a few short weeks it becomes nearly impossible to safely change the battery pack and supply the implant with a consistent flow of power. I fear that if we cannot get these test subjects under control or cannot find a new way to power these implants that we may never be able to fully and safely train these zombies. Since we have been d_____ the extra funding to _____ he implants, we are forced to _____ way to teach the ZED to c_____

The 26 Signs of the Zombie Apocalypse

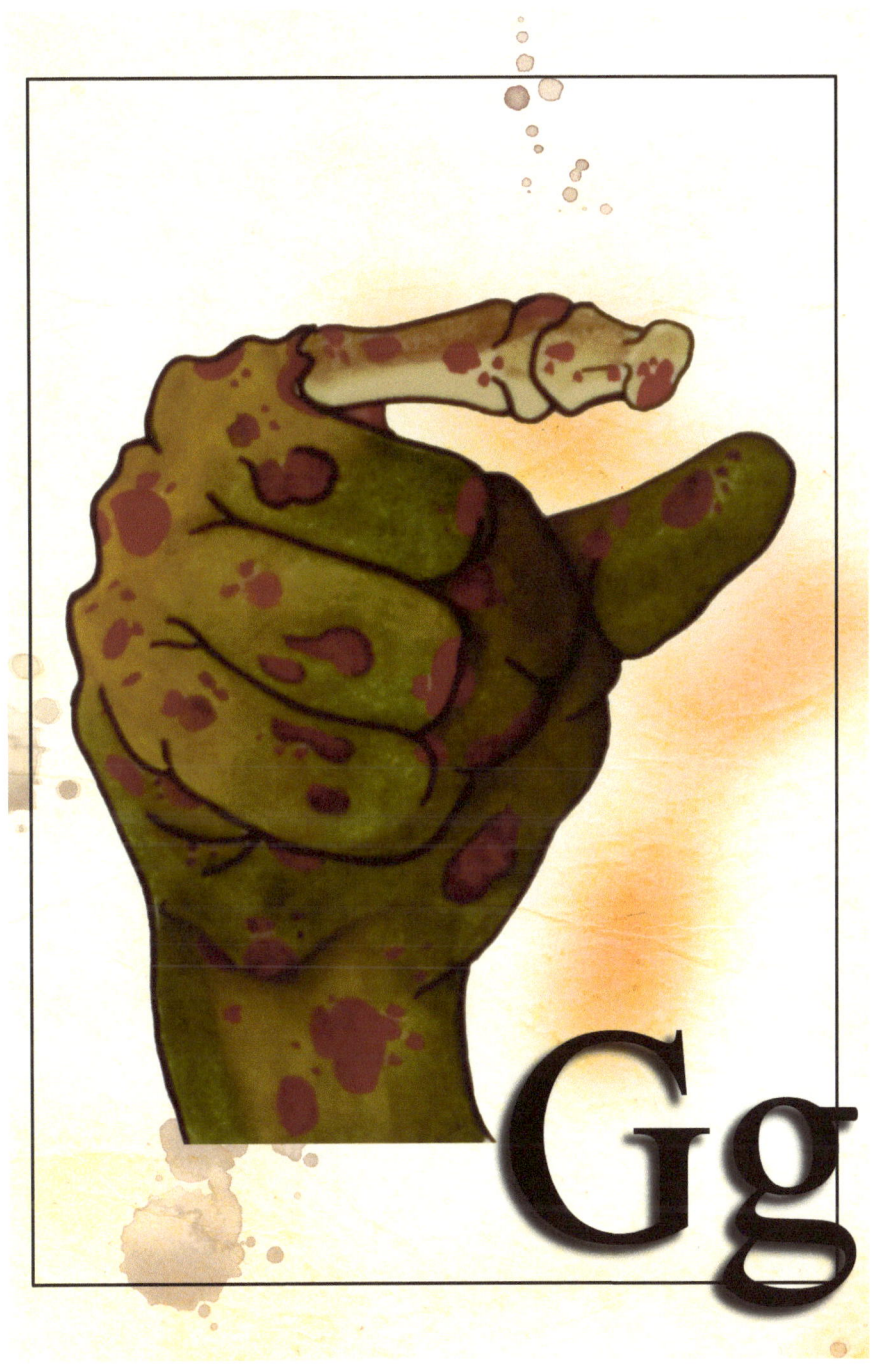

Gg

15 Feb 1976,
In order to improve cooperation from test subjects we have decided to infect each testee only after a fasting period of 48 hours. Reasoning for this is simple. We want these ZED t_____ y immediately after infection. H_____ ms to be the driving force behind the infected and we feel that we _an ____
throug____
train__

The Dr. was correct in his assumption that the Zed get hungrier and more feral as time goes on. We have discovered that the zombies can in fact die after a long enough span without food. We still don't know exactly how long it takes. We have only recently started to find truly dead corpses. This must be when Dr. Huss changed the original infection method to include fasting. He was also right about the zombies being more food oriented than anything else. In fact there doesn't seem to be any other driving force for the undead horde at all. The Lazarus virus requires it's host to ingest unbelievable amounts of living flesh. We have watched zombies continue to feast even after their abdomen bursts.

The 26 Signs of the Zombie Apocalypse

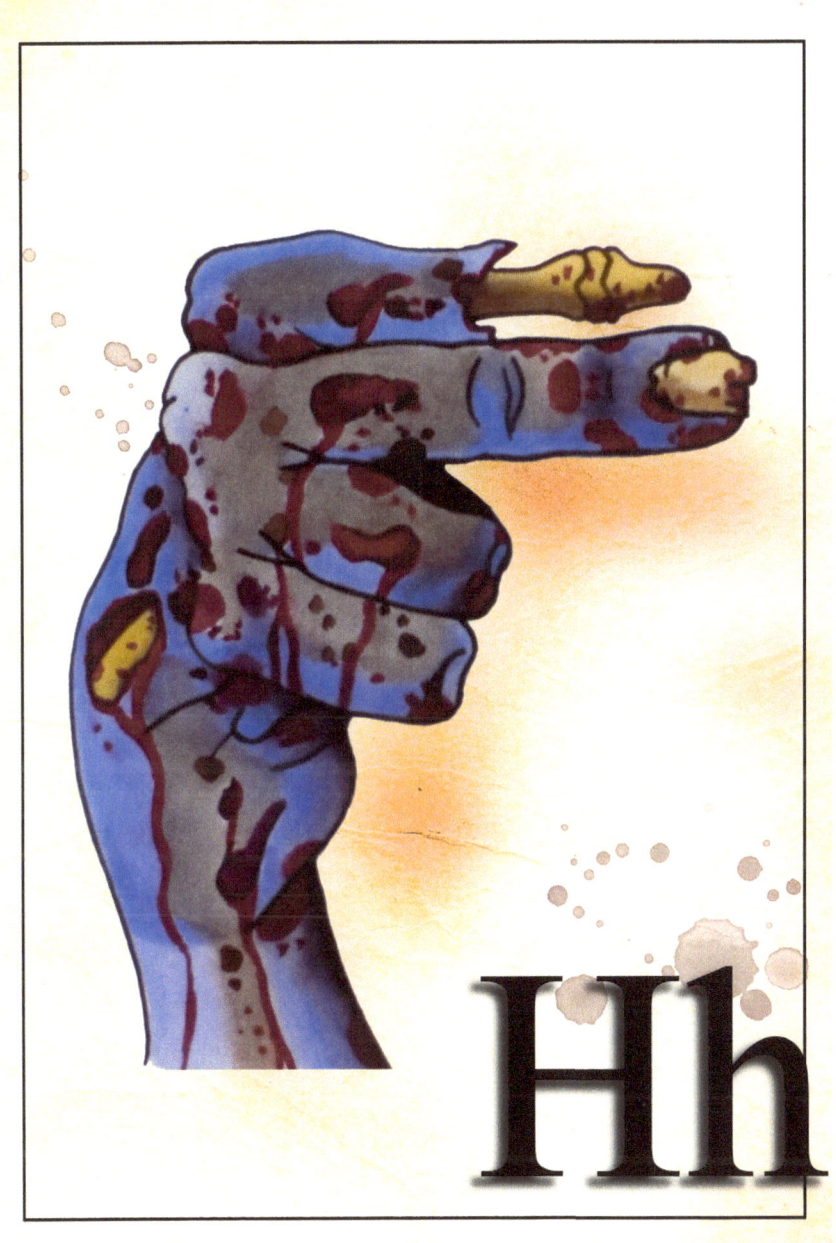

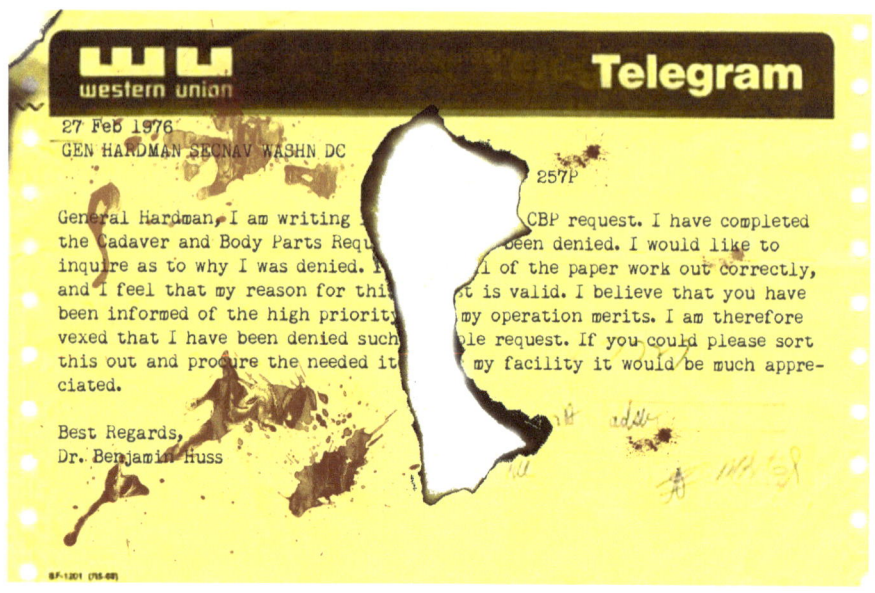

It seems strange that with a project like this being so obviously hidden from the public eye Dr. Huss still had to use normal channels for some of his supplies. We can only assume that this whole operation was not internal. As we can see here, body parts and cadavers had to be acquired through outside sources. Most of which came from a company in Louisville KY. Could you imagine being one of the poor souls who decides to donate your body to science upon your death thinking that it will help cure cancer and you end up there, in the belly of a Zed. Most of us don't even feel like the normal world ever existed. It seems so far away.

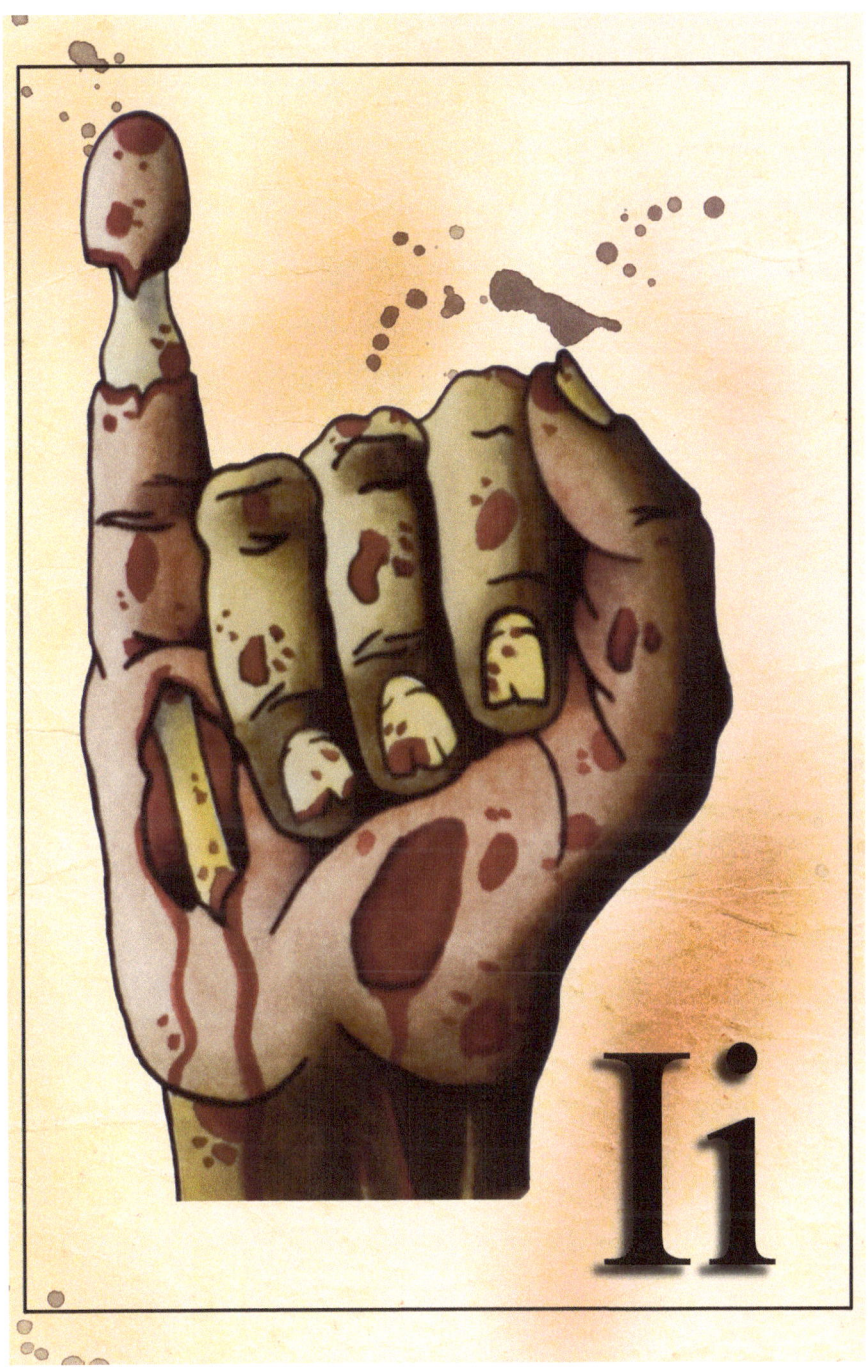

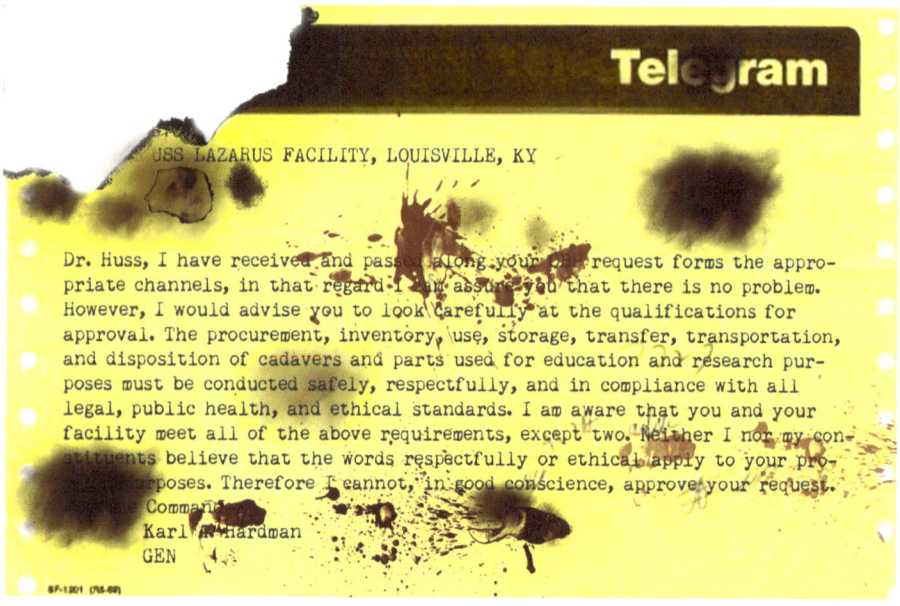

So far we have been unable to understand the relationship between General Hardman and Dr. Huss other than the fact they don't seem to like each other very much. Perhaps they were in the military together as I can't imagine that a normal doctor would ever volunteer for this project. Maybe he was drafted into it. In my opinion, General Hardman is the only person in this whole scenario that has any sense. He makes it very clear that he does not agree with any of these experiments and does everything he can do to stand in the way of Dr. Huss' success. Maybe if the general had had the power over the lab he could have stopped all of this from ever happening and we wouldn't have to raise our children in a world were being a Suicide Squad member is a valid career option.

The 26 Signs of the Zombie Apocalypse

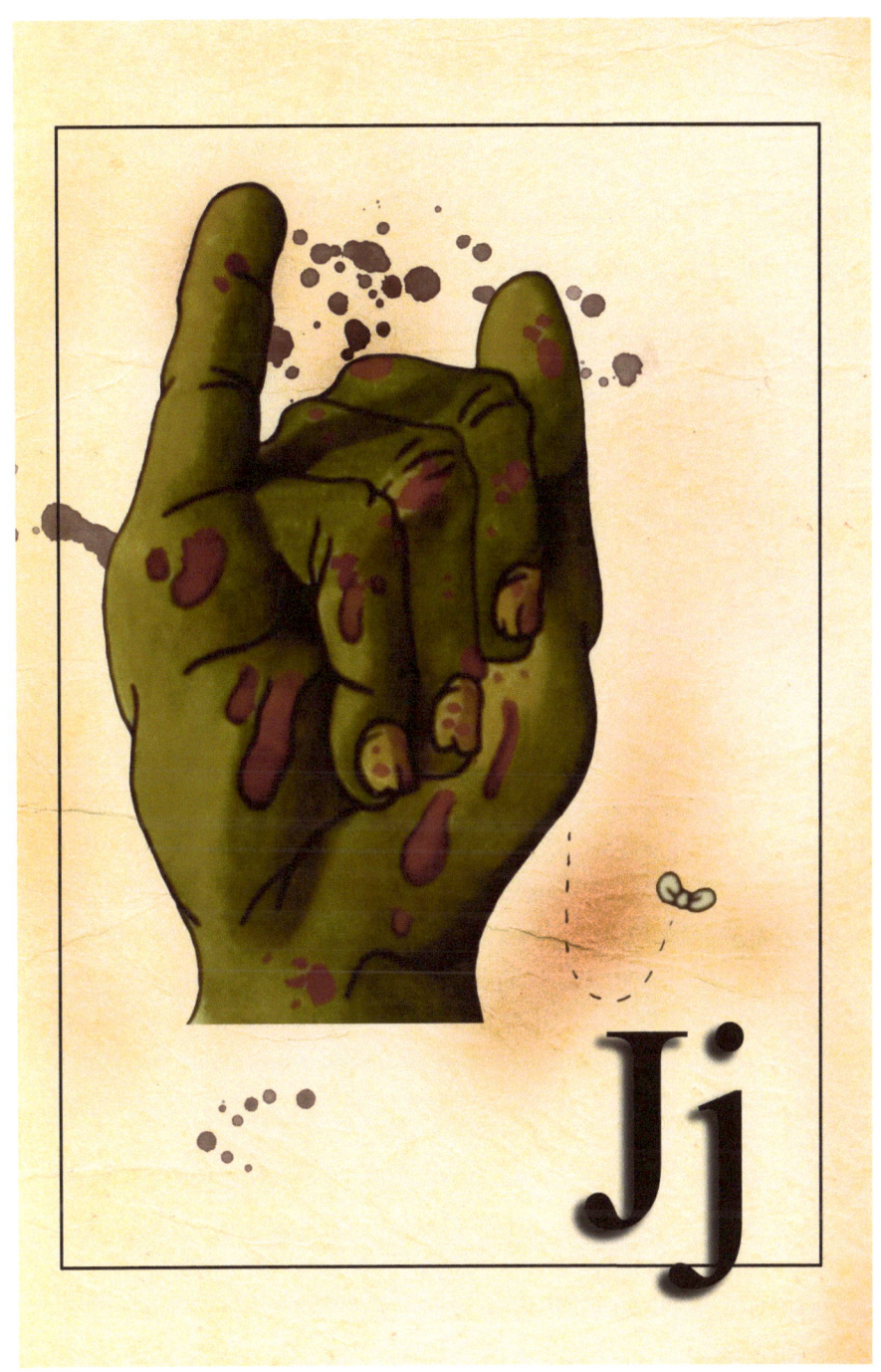

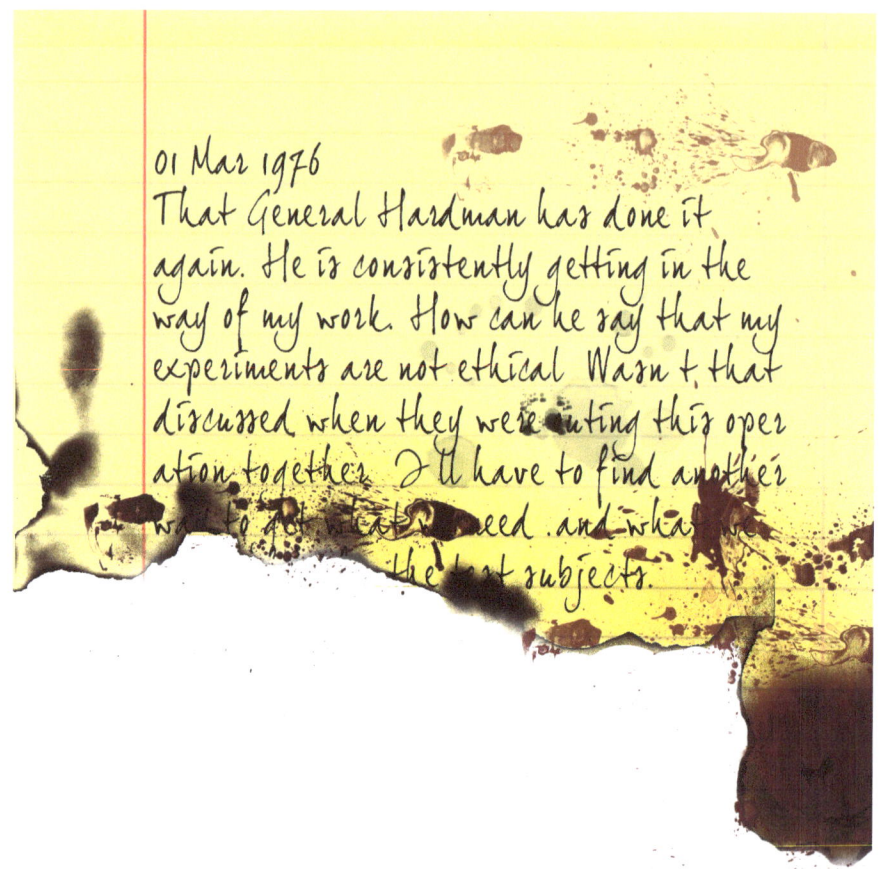

01 Mar 1976
That General Hardman has done it again. He is consistently getting in the way of my work. How can he say that my experiments are not ethical. Wasn't that discussed when they were cutting this oper ation together. I'll have to find another w... eed. and wha... the ... t subjects.

We are not exactly sure what Dr. Huss needed the cadavers for. The most obvious reason is for the arms. He needed cadaver hands for his experiments as stated previously. I speculate that he was also trying to reanimate these corpses as a control group to compare to the living infected. There are others though who believe the worst. Dr. Benjamin Huss wanted to feed them to the zombies.

This shouldn't be a huge surprise considering that everyone knows Zed eat people. We also know that they prefer living flesh to dead. Freshly dead in a pinch.

The 26 Signs of the Zombie Apocalypse

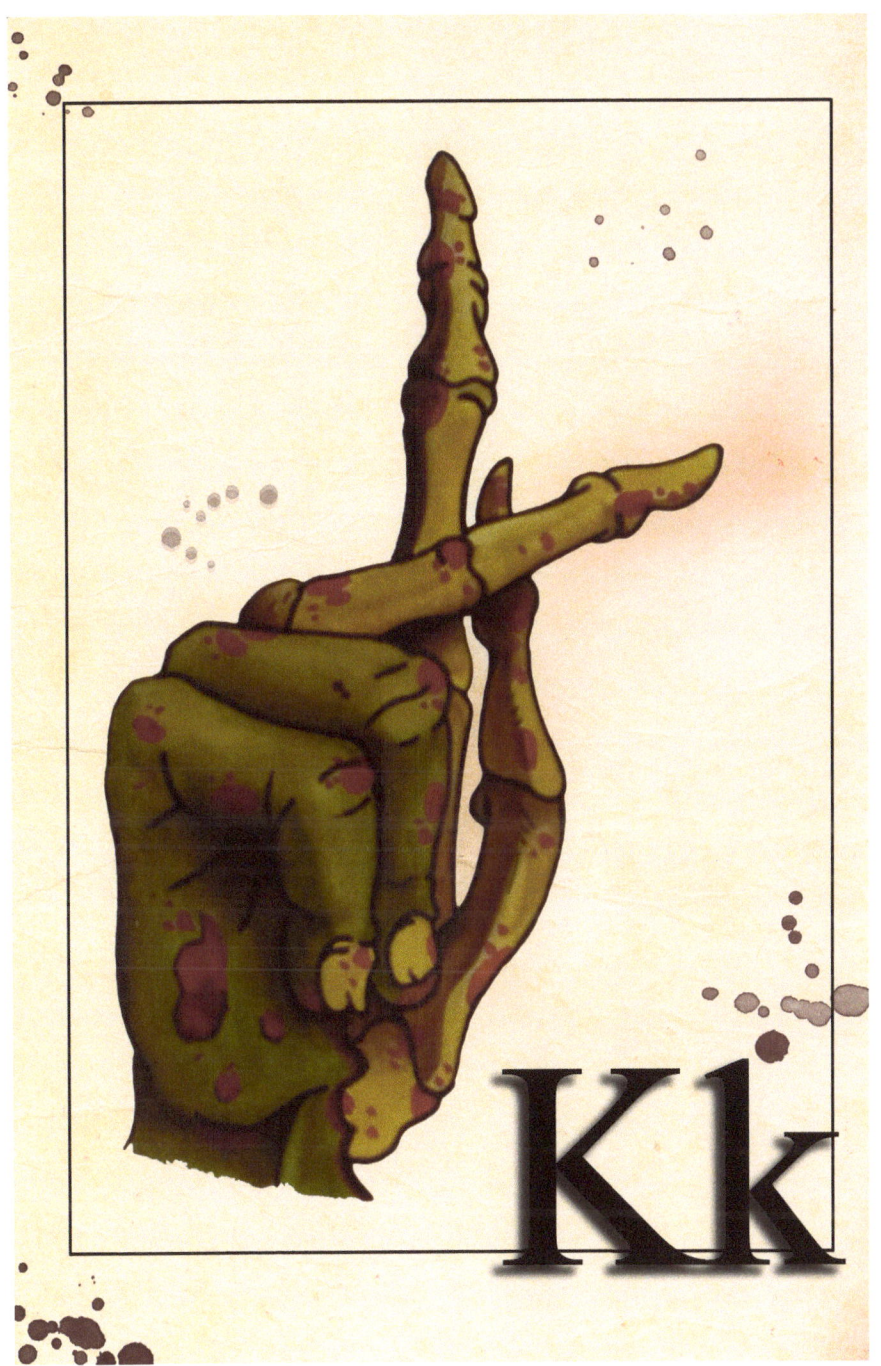

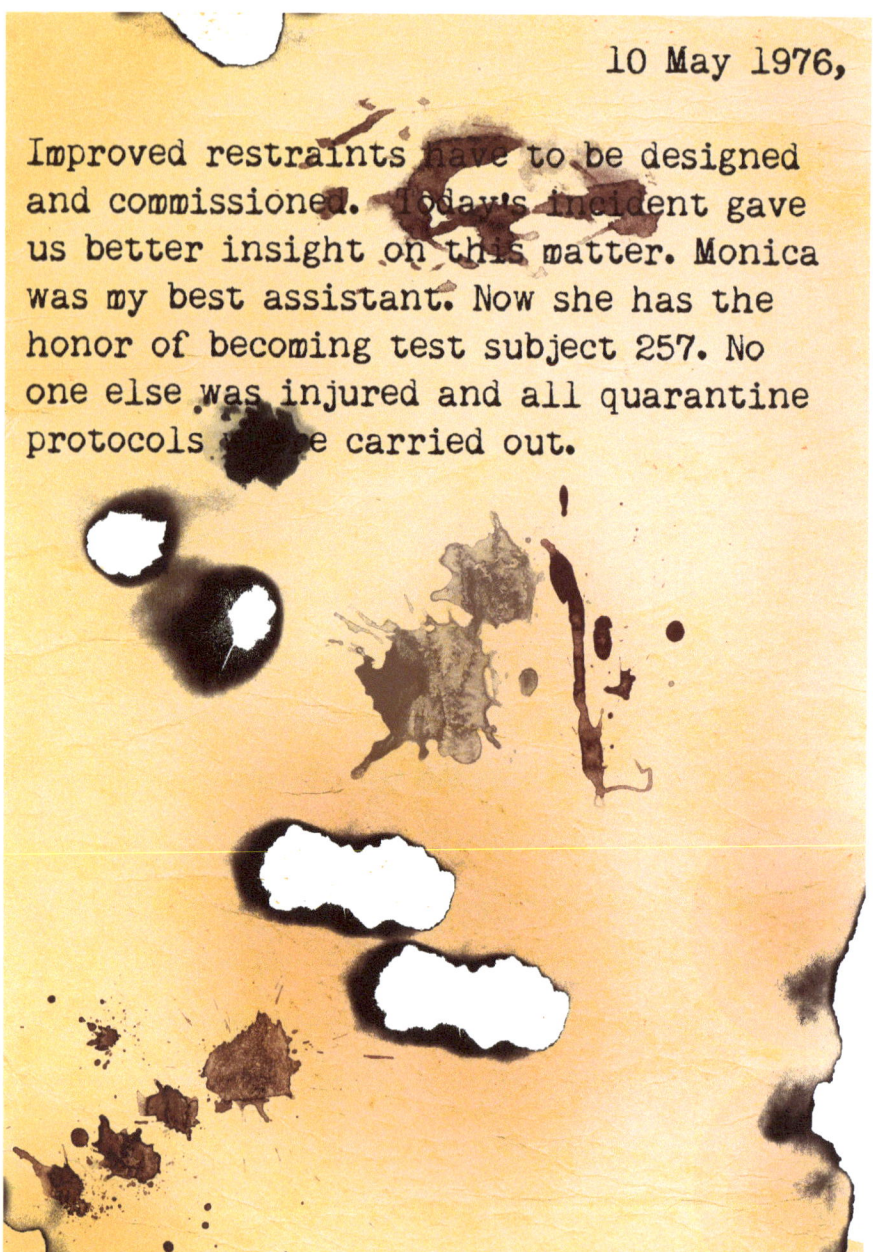

10 May 1976,

Improved restraints have to be designed and commissioned. Today's incident gave us better insight on this matter. Monica was my best assistant. Now she has the honor of becoming test subject 257. No one else was injured and all quarantine protocols were carried out.

The 26 Signs of the Zombie Apocalypse

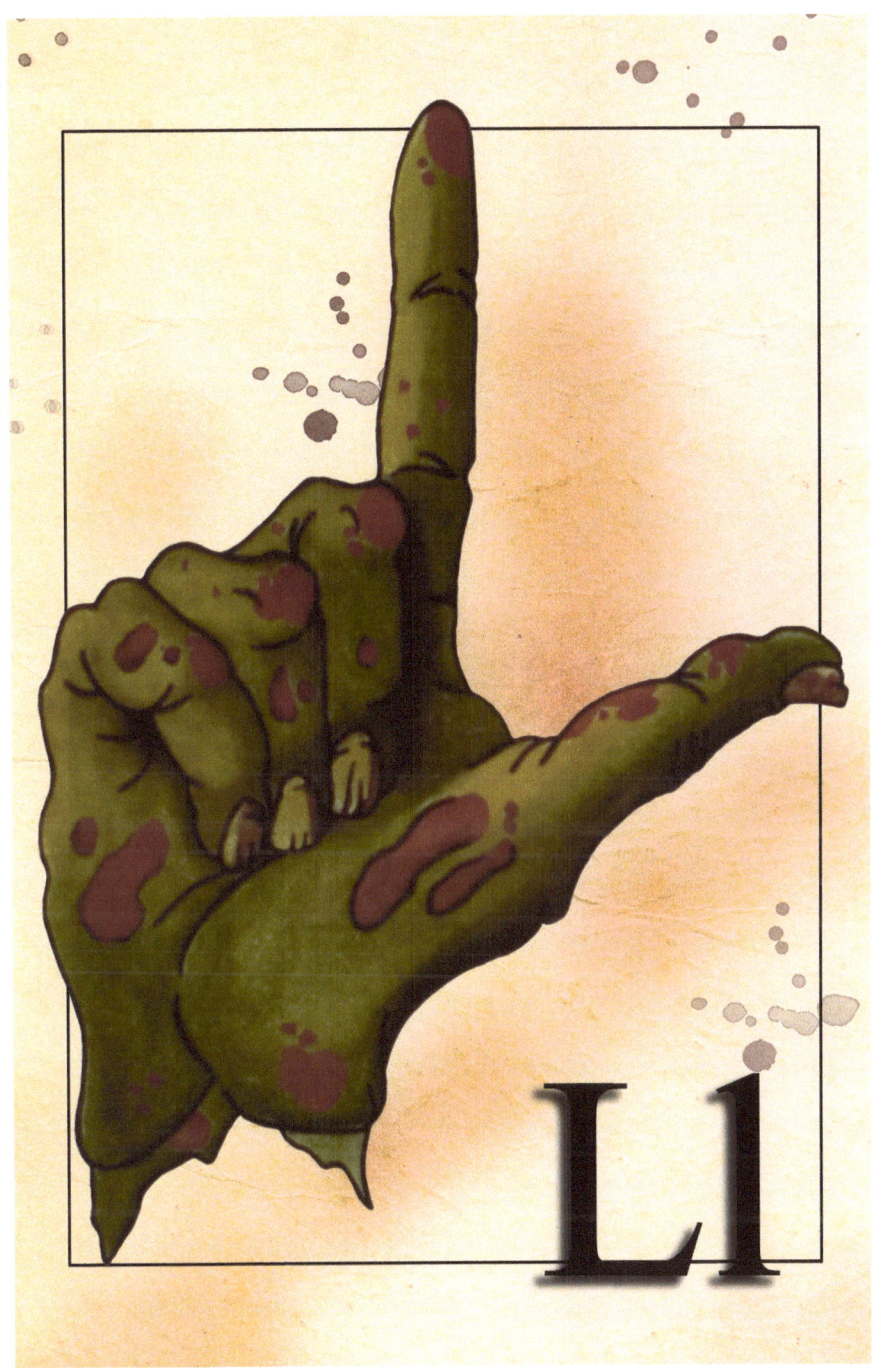

> 24 Jun 19█
>
> Through even more █ompetence shown by my team of ex██ scientists we have discovered some█████ng extraordinary. Test subject 78, █████ one of our oldest and most decaye█ █ubjects, was cut in half. During a routine cue card sess███, the laboratory assistant in the █████ with number 78 got too close and was attacked. The assistant ran out of the room and in an attempt to prevent contamination of the facility, the door was closed even though the ZED was onl█ █rtial1y through the door. This process left 78's torso on the outside of the enclosure while his lower half remained inside. I had one of our expert surgeons, Dr. Jerromy, restore ZED 78, but I have little hope that he will █████ val██ab1e test s██ject. Such a

We assume that the extraordinary part was that the Zed remained "alive" even after he had been detached from his lower body.

The 26 Signs of the Zombie Apocalypse

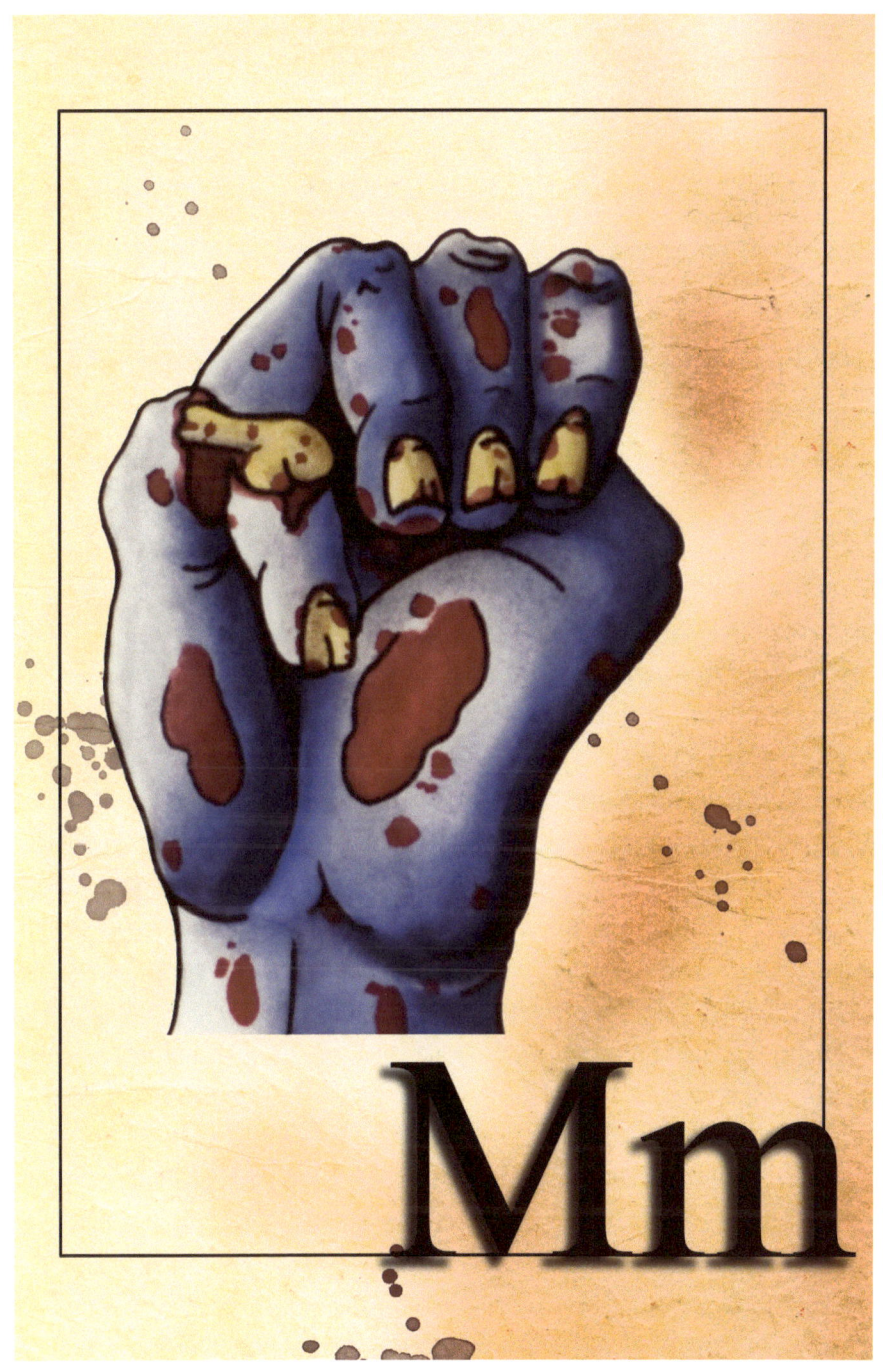

Mm

> 25 Jun 1976
>
> It's a miracle! 78 has already begun to walk again! I already knew that ZED could withstand significant trauma to the central nervous system, but this is unprecedented. We must do more research into the phenomenon for the good of mankind... unlock this mechanism

Had Dr. Huss not been so naive to the dangers that Zed posed to mankind this incident would have terrified him. The good doctor viewed this scenario through the eyes of a person looking to cure the world of paralysis and hardship. While his intentions were good and he obviously didn't see the danger involved. It is because f the undead's ability to function long after living tissue fails that the human race is on the brink of extinction.

If Dr. Huss had looked closely he would have noticed that yet again, this "miracle" had nothing to do with the body of his test subject at all. This is simply a way for the virus to survive. Zombies do not have the ability to heal at all. They don't need it. We often see zombies that are missing vital organs or limbs and they continue to thrive. As long as the brain is intact the Zed can continue on as if nothing were wrong. This test subject simply began walking again because his body was sewn back together allowing the virus to continue using the lower half of the body as it had done before. This is what makes the Zed so difficult to kill.

The 26 Signs of the Zombie Apocalypse

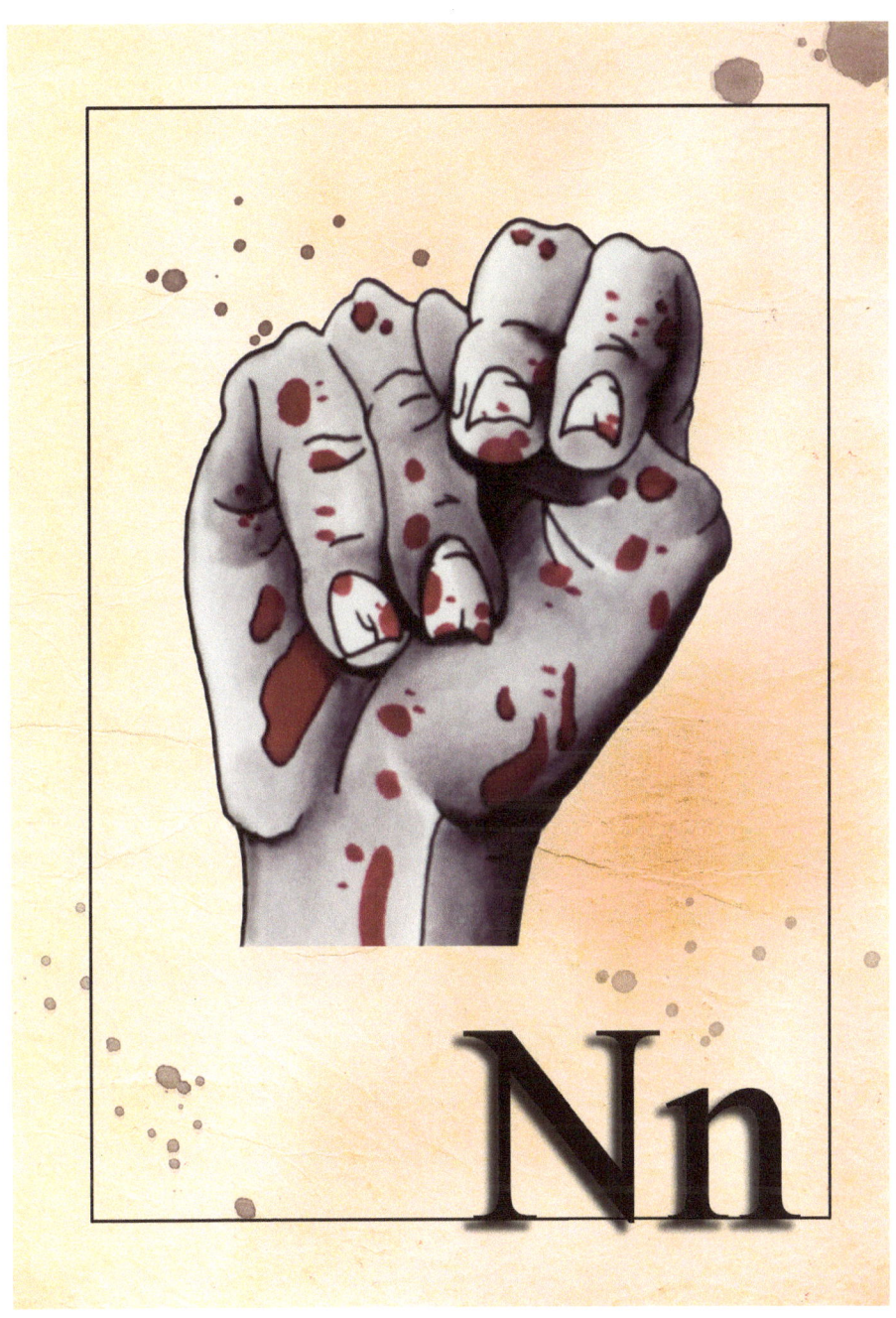

Nn

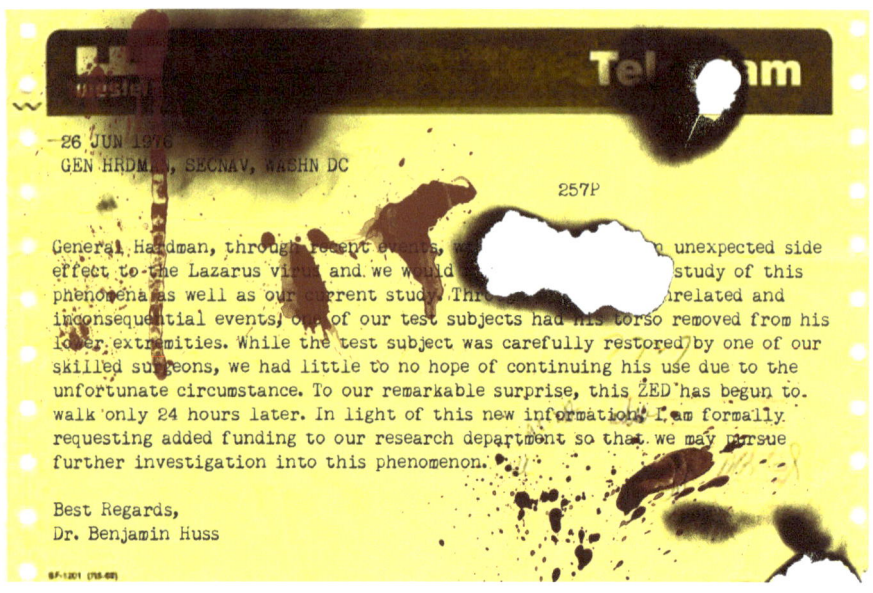

Yet again our doctor continues to hold on to hopes that the undead can somehow be studied and put to use helping humanity, and once again he is wrong. There is no foe so dangerous as a foe with nothing to lose. The Zed have nothing to lose. When you hurt them, they don't back down, when you intimidate them, they don't respond. Nothing stops them but the complete and total destruction of the brain. You can tear them apart, set them on fire, crush them, electrocute them or shoot them. It doesn't matter unless you exploit the one and only weakness they have. The virus controls the body and the virus needs the brain to do this. You destroy the brain. Nothing else matters.

The 26 Signs of the Zombie Apocalypse

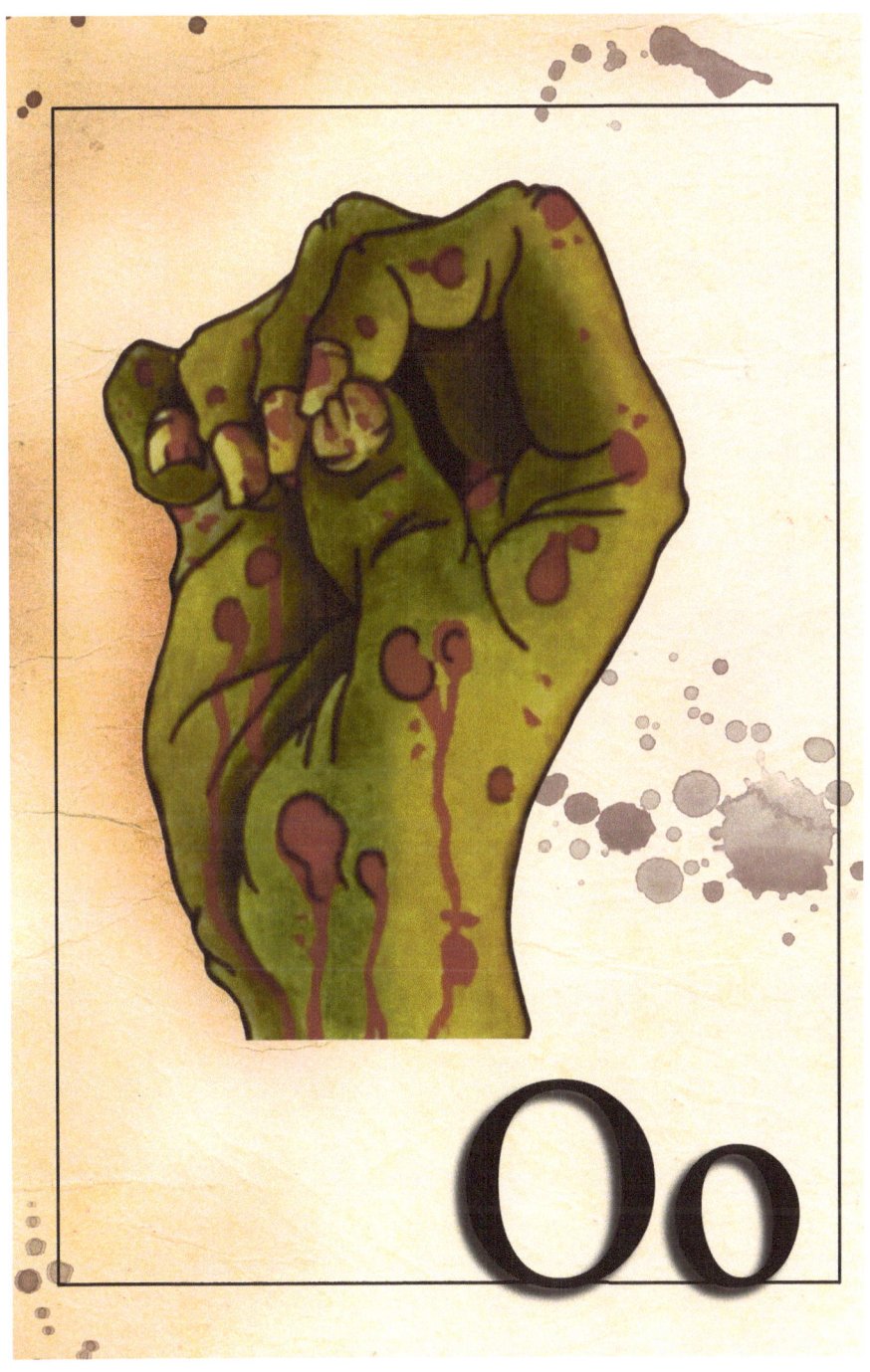

Oo

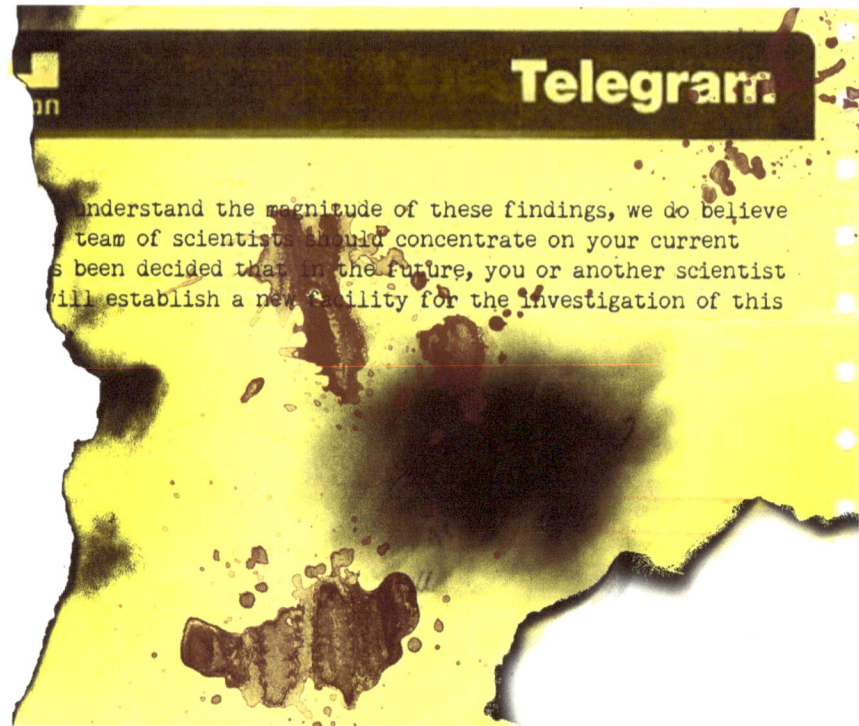

This telegram was badly damaged and is hard to read, but I believe the General was yet again denying Dr. Huss in his request to investigate the healing properties of his miracle test subject. This was both good and bad. Good because it prevented more interest in the research of the Lazarus virus. Bad because the doctor might have discovered the connection between the virus and the brain earlier than we did therefore saving many lives. If we would have known about the brain being the only weak point sooner we may have even been able to prevent the collapse of human civilization all together. We might have been able to exterminate the undead threat before it became too widespread to correct. Unfortunately the human race had never encountered something that could out murder us before. We had certainly never seen anything that could convert us into more ferocious killing machines than we already were as a species.

The 26 Signs of the Zombie Apocalypse

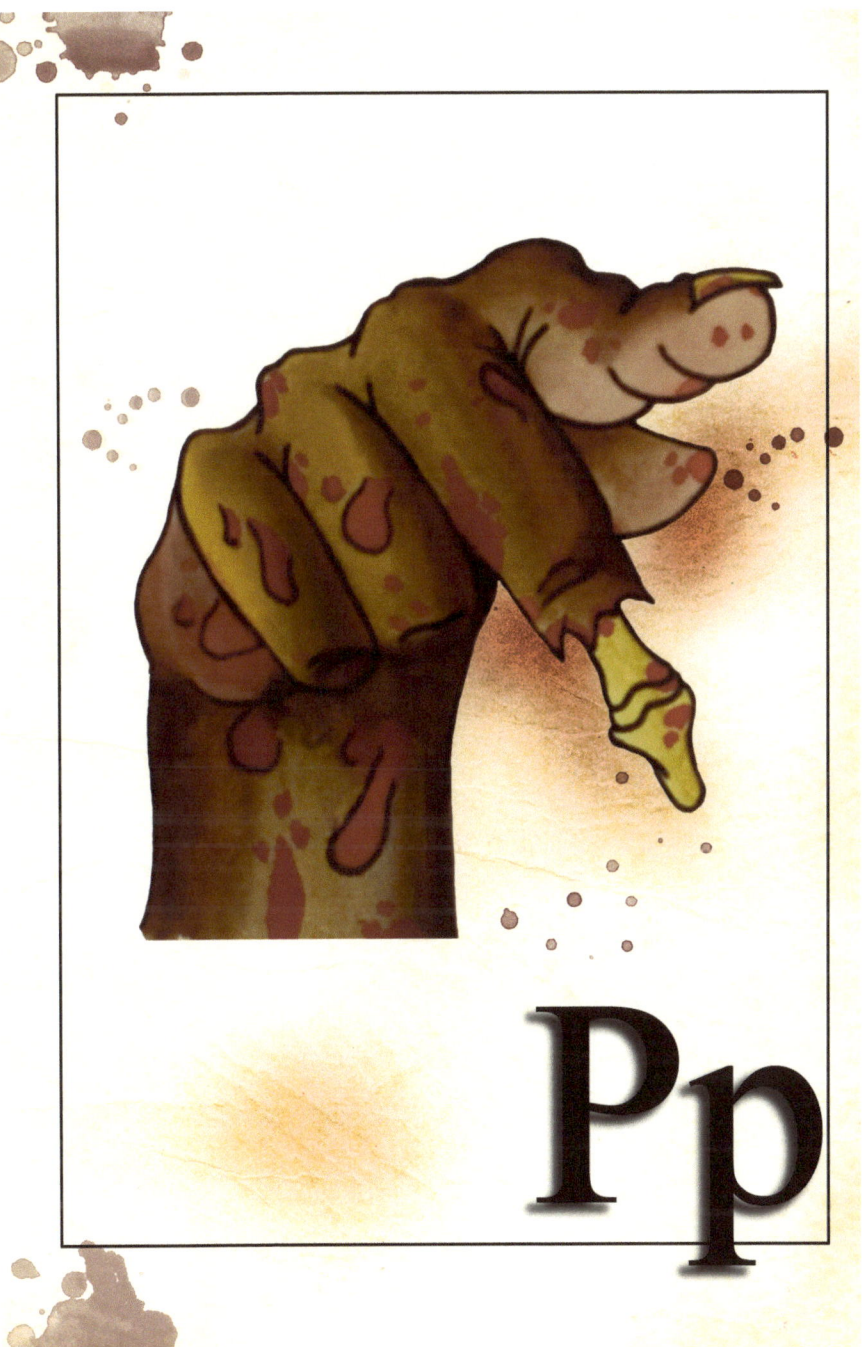

Pp

25 Jul 1976,

Test subject 257 is progressing far beyond any of the other subjects. Perhaps her time spent as a lab assistant makes her a better candidate. Her higher levels of intelligence and social skill may be lingering beyond death.

The 26 Signs of the Zombie Apocalypse

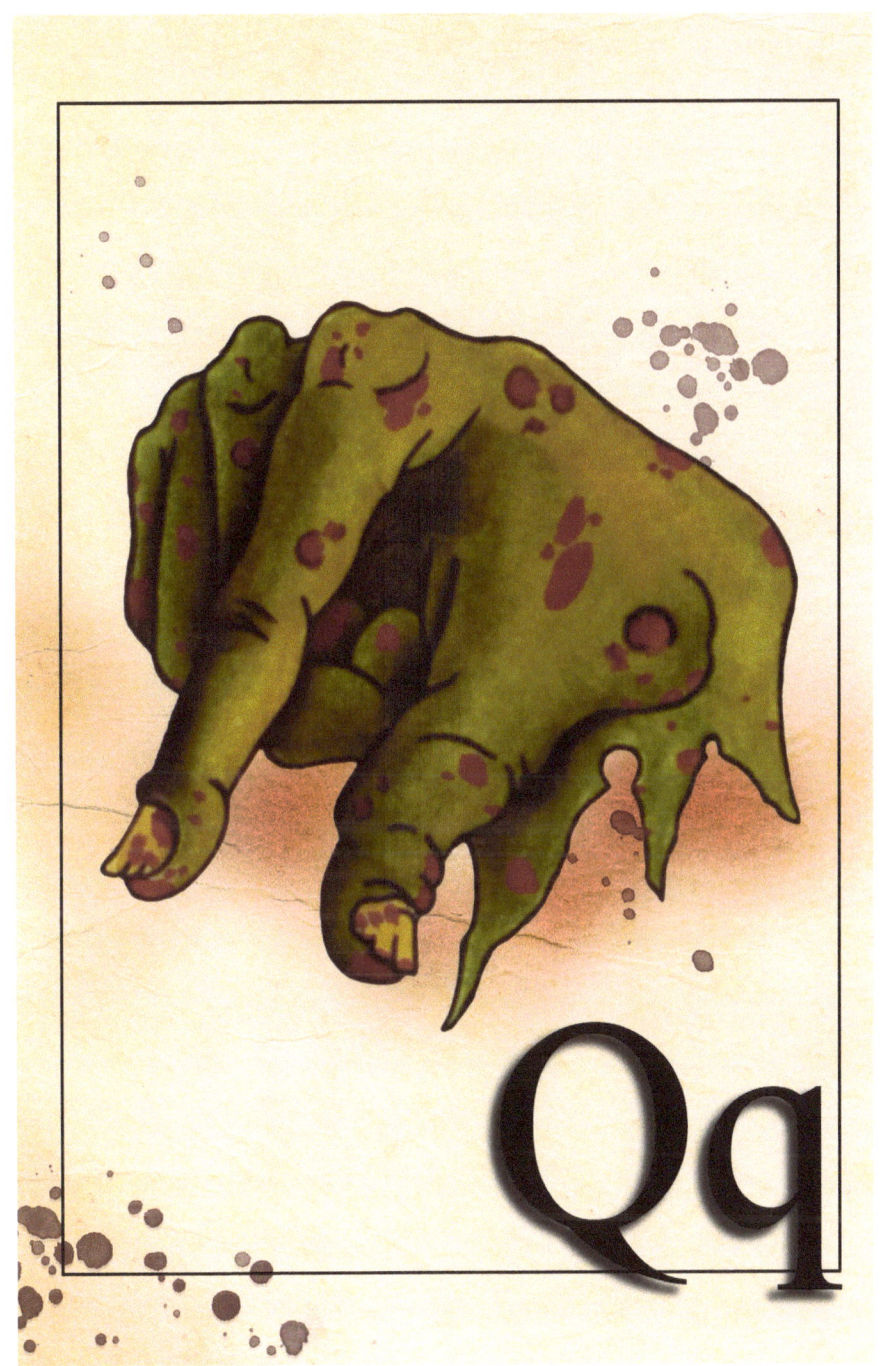

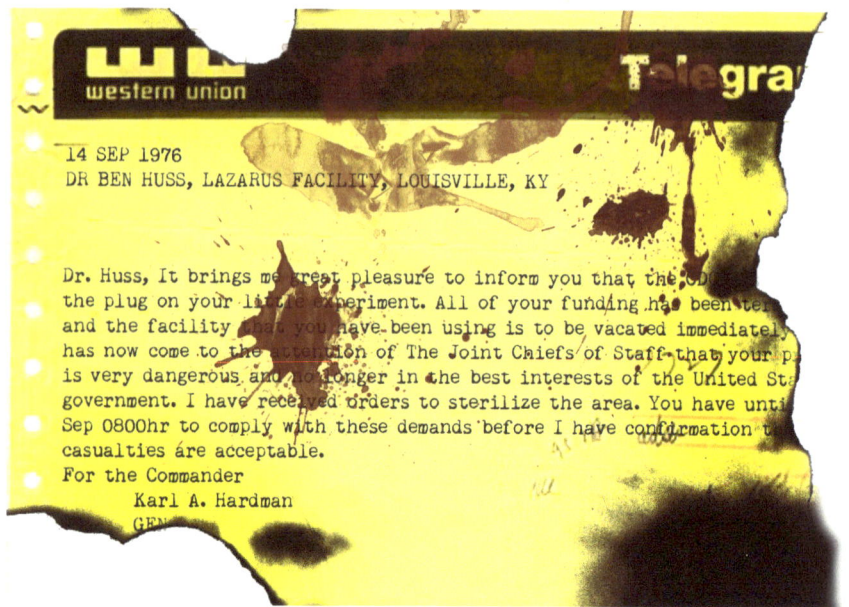

I don't understand what took our government so long to come to it's senses. We can only speculate that ending this project sooner might have prevented the virus from spreading, but in all reality that is probably not true. I can' imagine being one of those people in the lab, being assigned to work on this project and then learning that you would be exterminated if you didn't evacuate in time. Dr. Huss had obviously become obsessive with his work at the lab. He ordered his lab assistants to stop evacuating and protect his work. Of course this just created more panic and we assume that this is when people became careless. Every person that worked in that lab was sentenced to death. The fear that those people experienced is evident in what they left behind, the messages on the walls, the journal entries of people saying goodbye to their loved ones. Some of the uninfected were even found in the cells with what we can only assume were their charges. If only they had known what was to become of mankind.

The 26 Signs of the Zombie Apocalypse

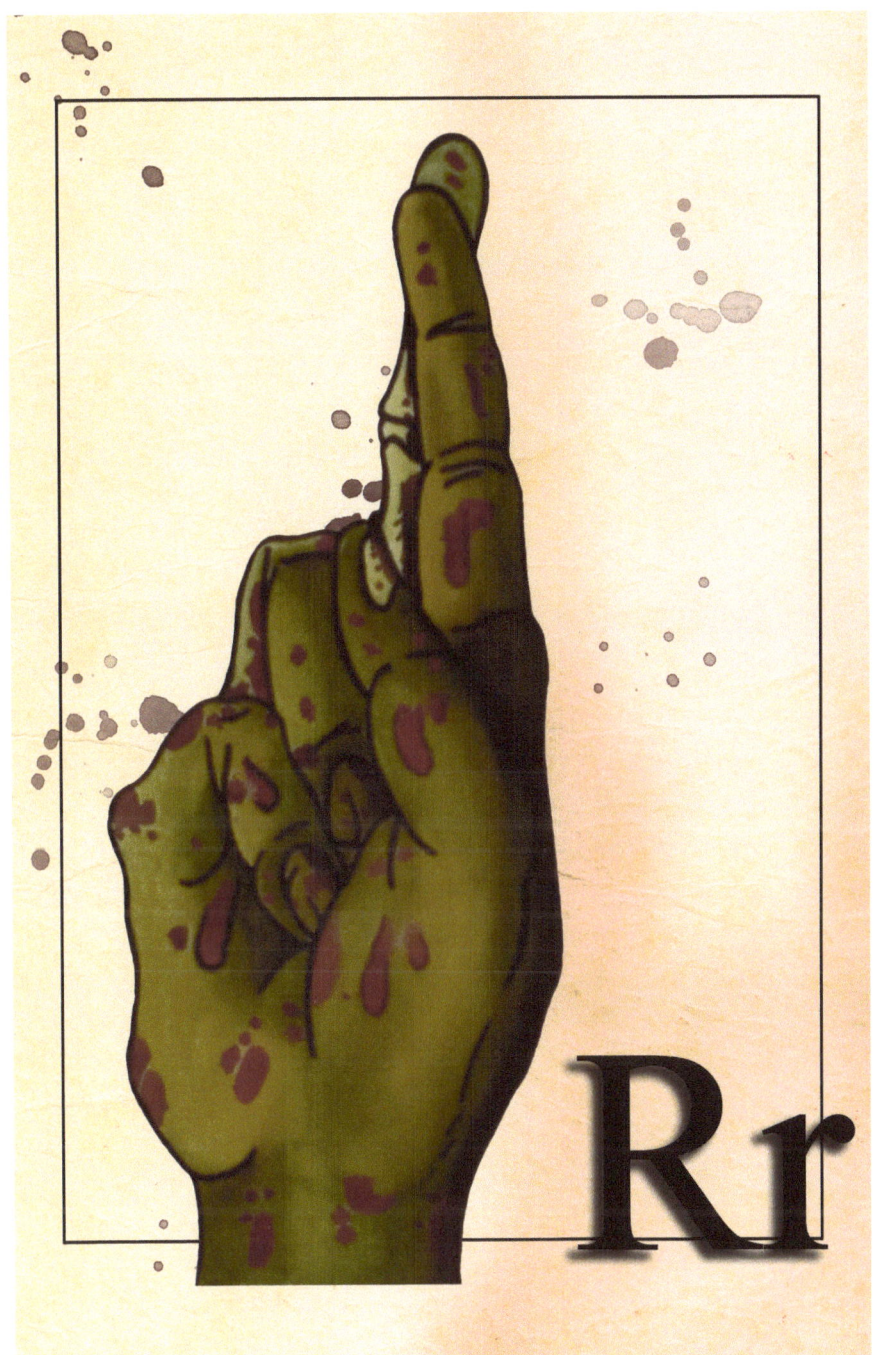

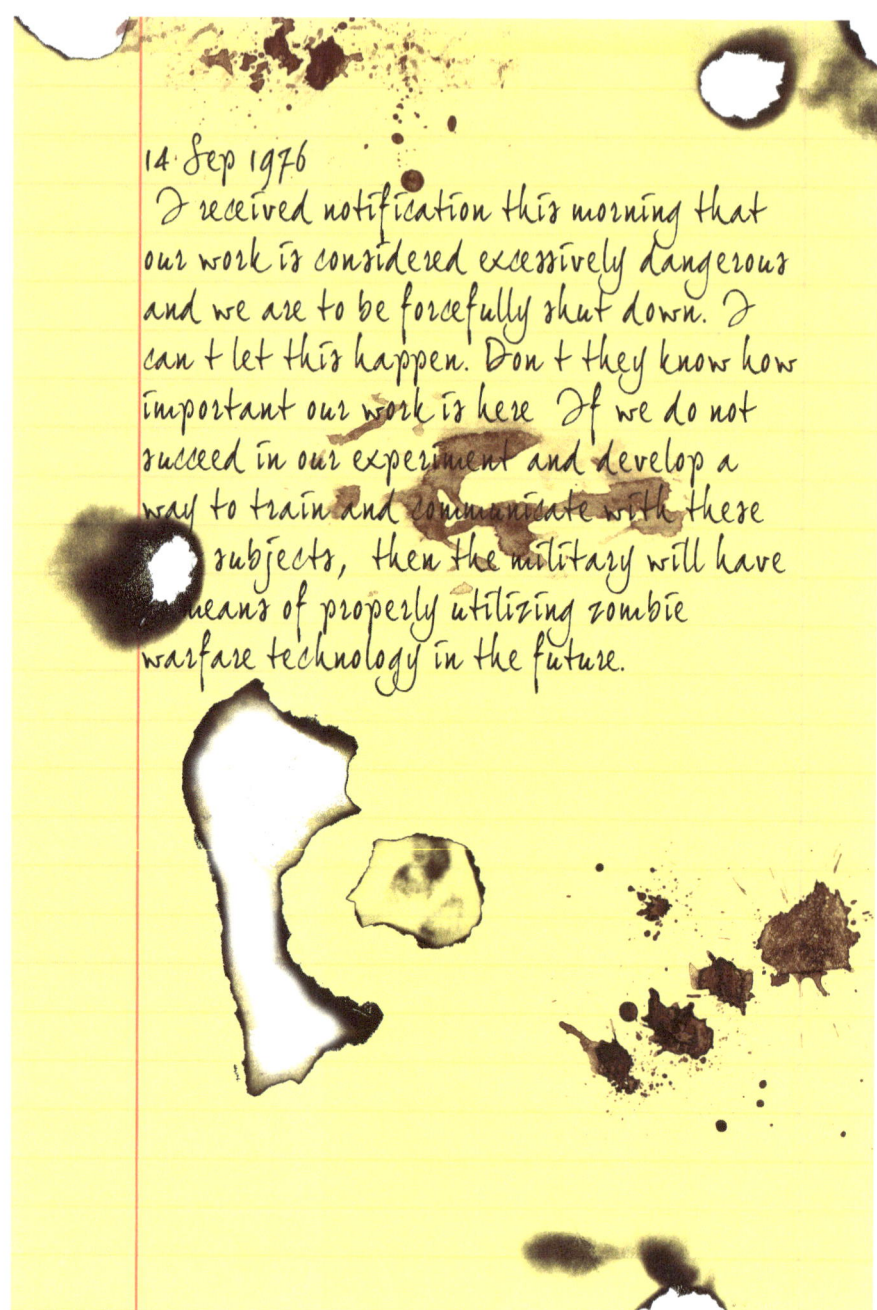

14 Sep 1976

I received notification this morning that our work is considered excessively dangerous and we are to be forcefully shut down. I can't let this happen. Don't they know how important our work is here. If we do not succeed in our experiment and develop a way to train and communicate with these subjects, then the military will have no means of properly utilizing zombie warfare technology in the future.

The 26 Signs of the Zombie Apocalypse

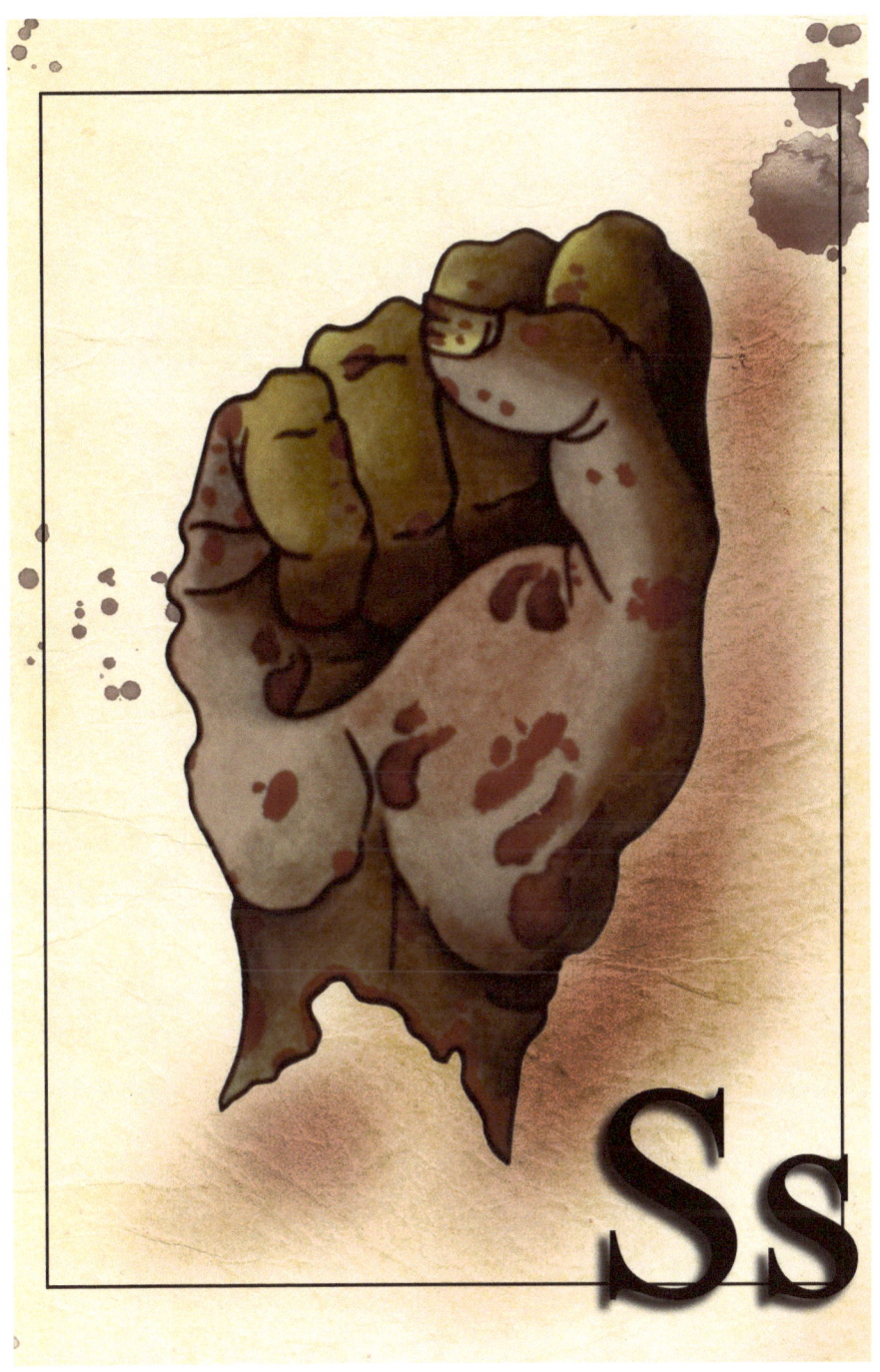

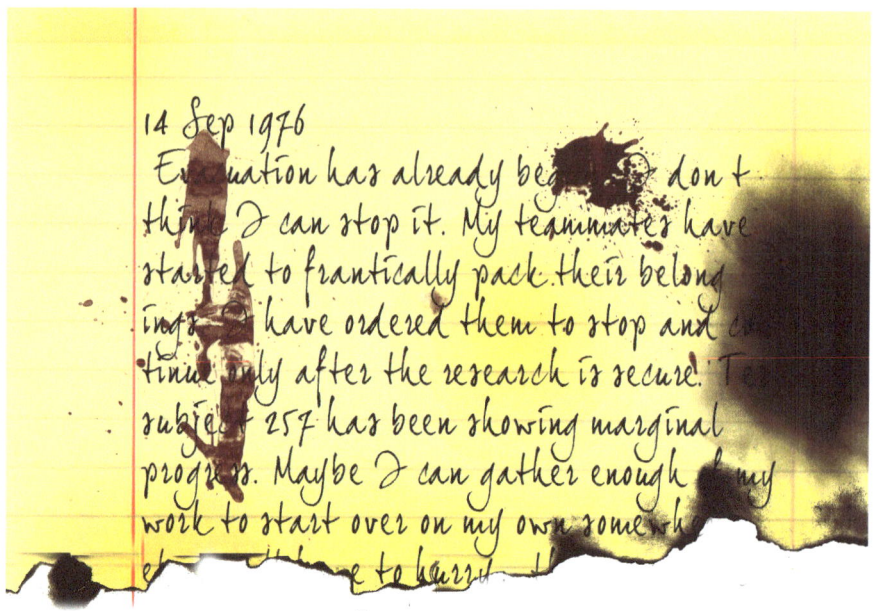

This is were it happened. In the panic. It's always panic. It stops you in your tracks and makes you stupid. That's the first thing we train out of our Suicide Squads. The ability to stay calm and think keeps you alive. We will send another Squad back to the lab and see if we can recover any more information, anything that will help us destroy this virus. Dr. Huss was right, they didn't destroy the Lazarus virus and it killed us. Not all of us, but most. It is now down to the few of human kind that remains. We have to stay calm, be smart and defend those borders that we still have left. We have to teach our children to think and act as if every moment is precious because it is. We have to think of our future generations. We can't afford to be greedy or righteous. We have been humbled as a species. We are no longer the top of the food chain. We are the hunted.

The 26 Signs of the Zombie Apocalypse

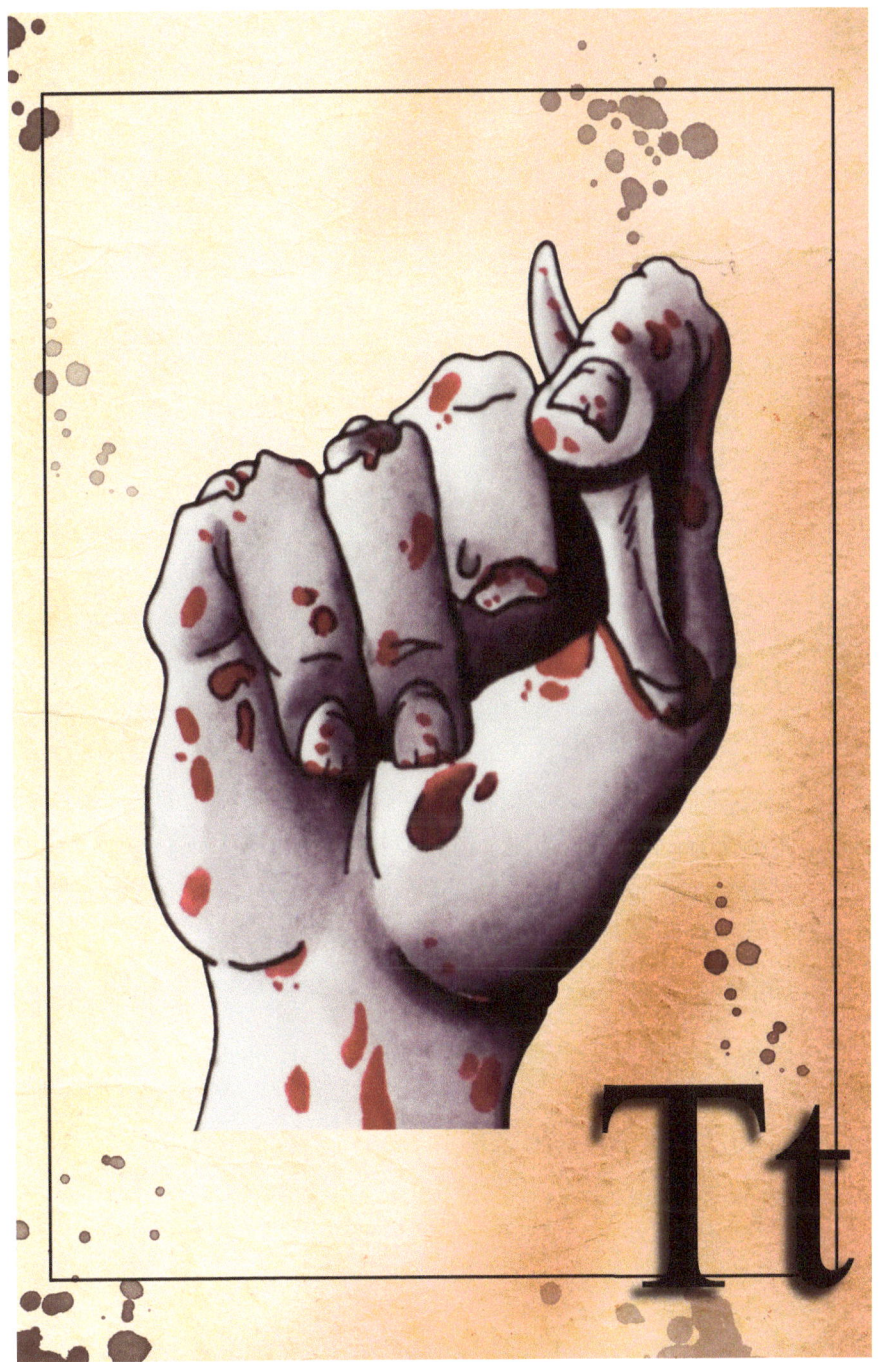

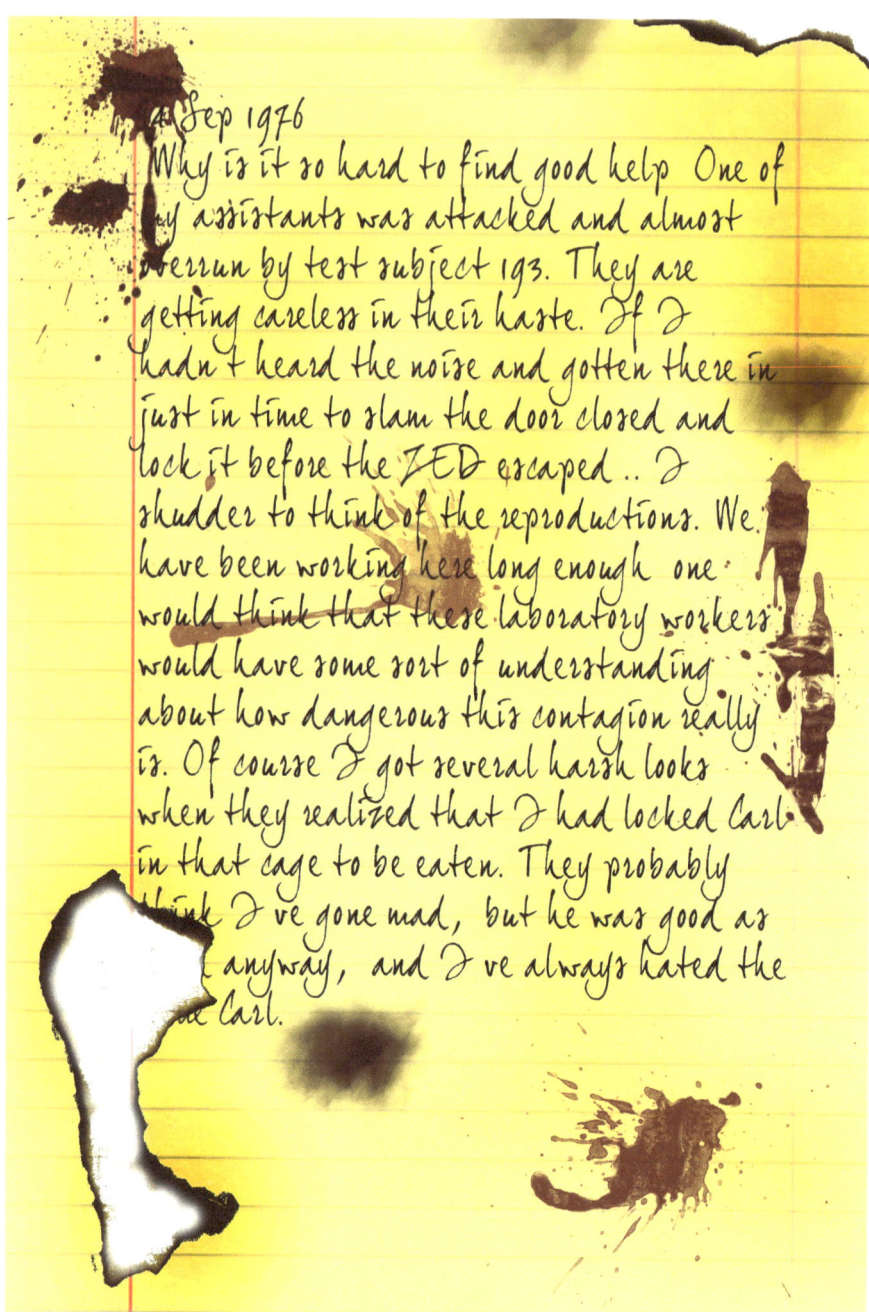

4 Sep 1976

Why is it so hard to find good help. One of my assistants was attacked and almost overrun by test subject 193. They are getting careless in their haste. If I hadn't heard the noise and gotten there in just in time to slam the door closed and lock it before the ZED escaped .. I shudder to think of the repercussions. We have been working here long enough one would think that these laboratory workers would have some sort of understanding about how dangerous this contagion really is. Of course I got several harsh looks when they realized that I had locked Carl in that cage to be eaten. They probably think I've gone mad, but he was good as ~~dead~~ anyway, and I've always hated the ~~name~~ Carl.

The 26 Signs of the Zombie Apocalypse

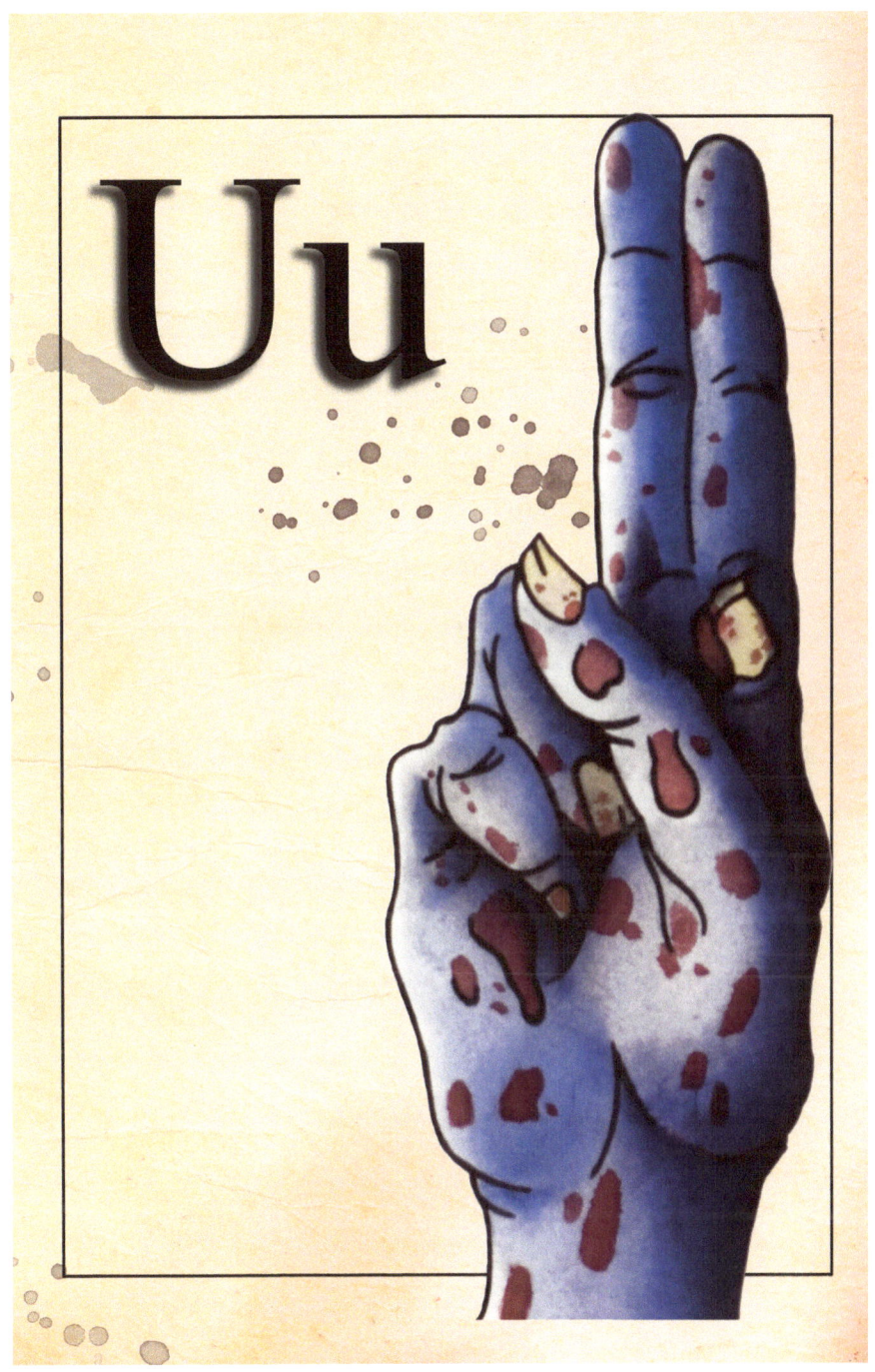

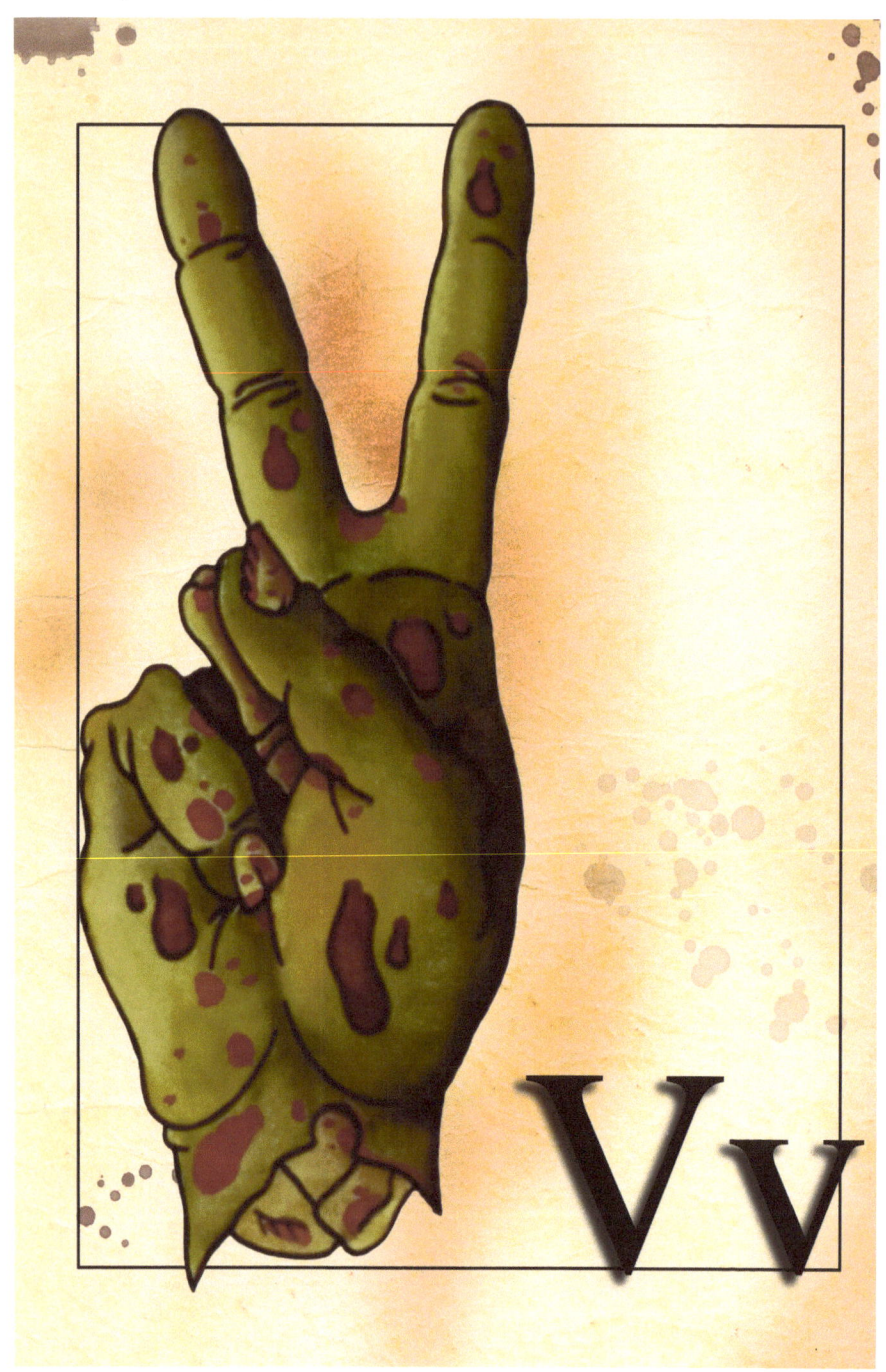

The 26 Signs of the Zombie Apocalypse

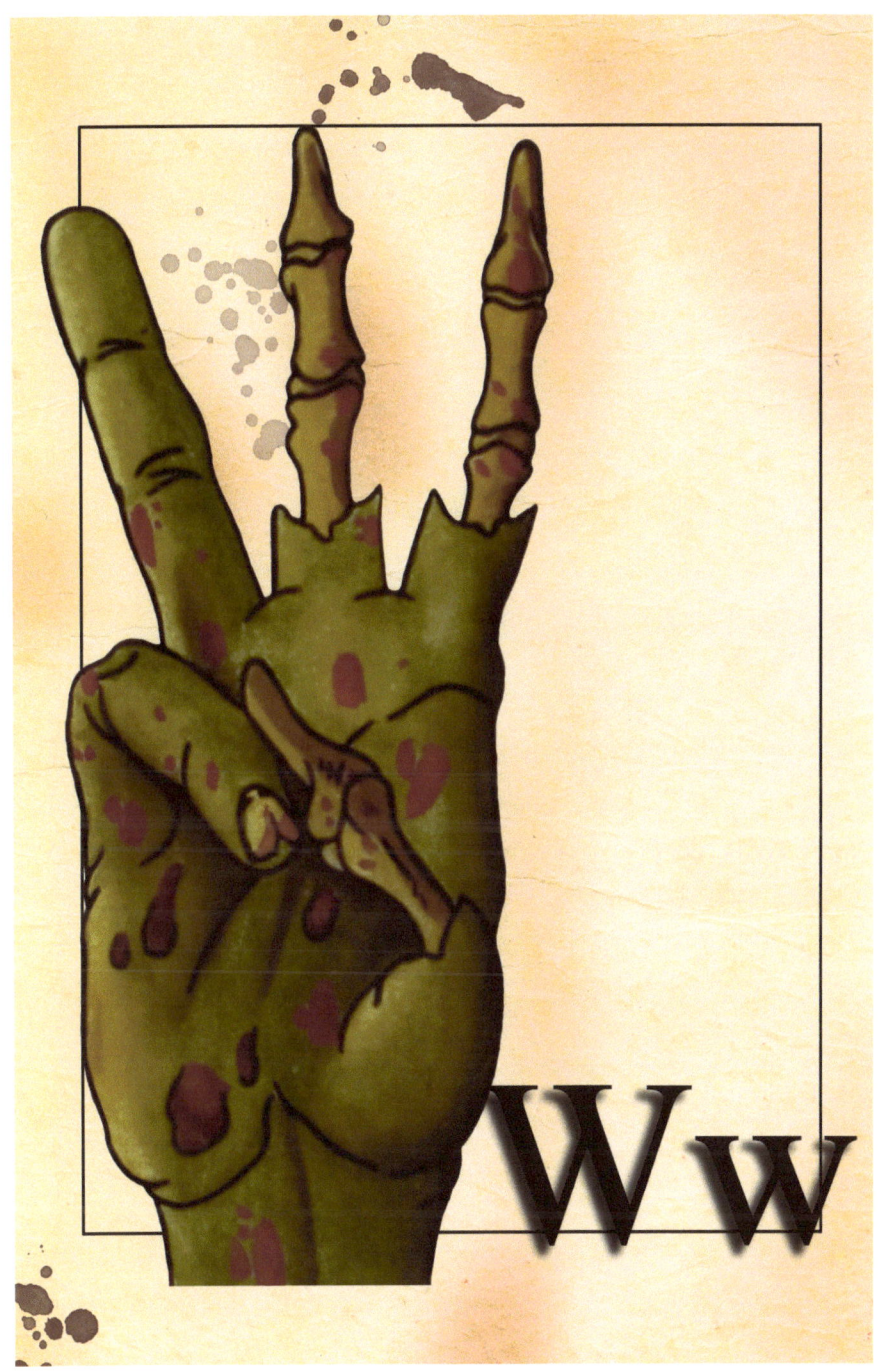

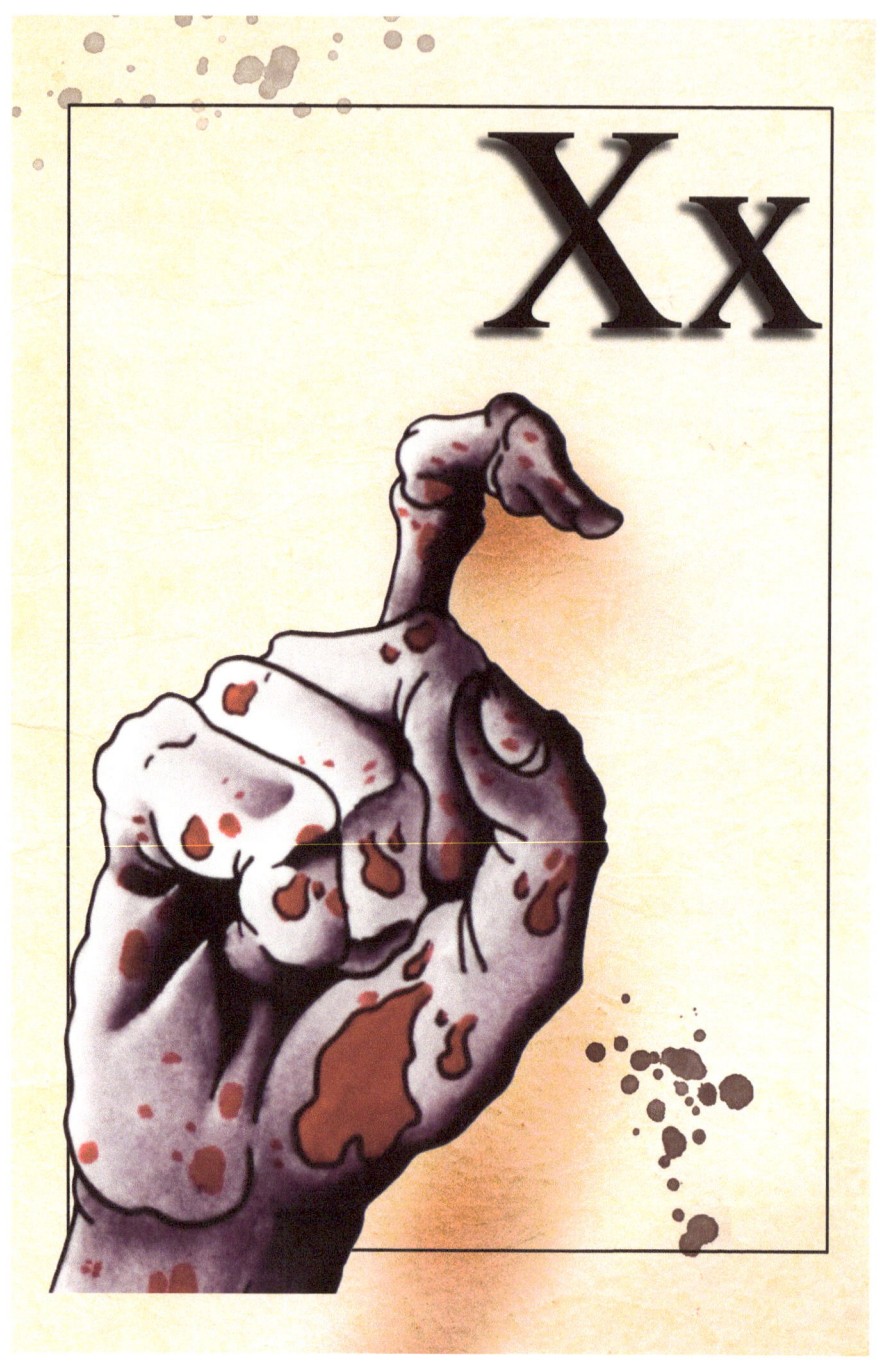

THE 26 SIGNS OF THE ZOMBIE APOCALYPSE

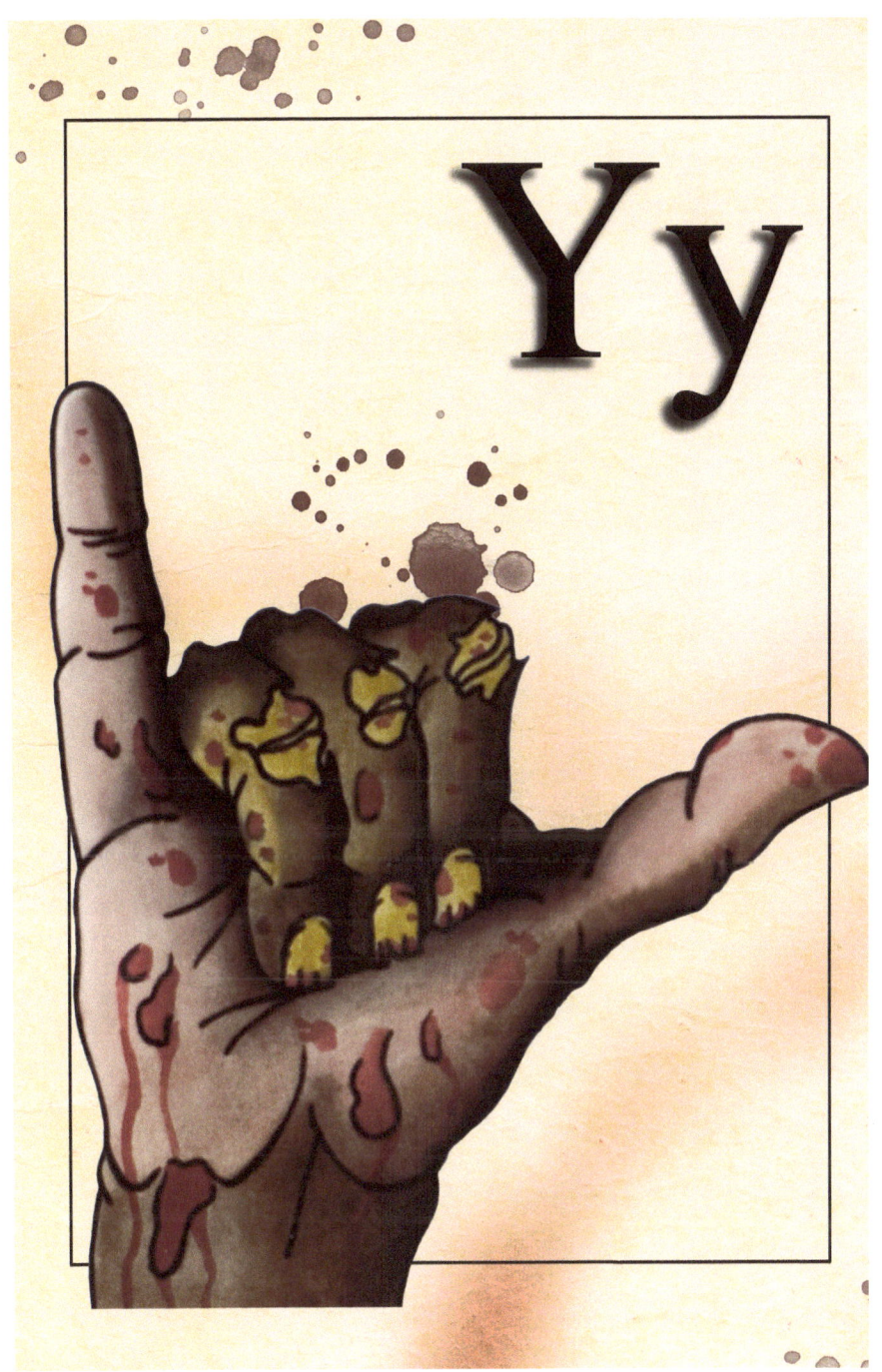

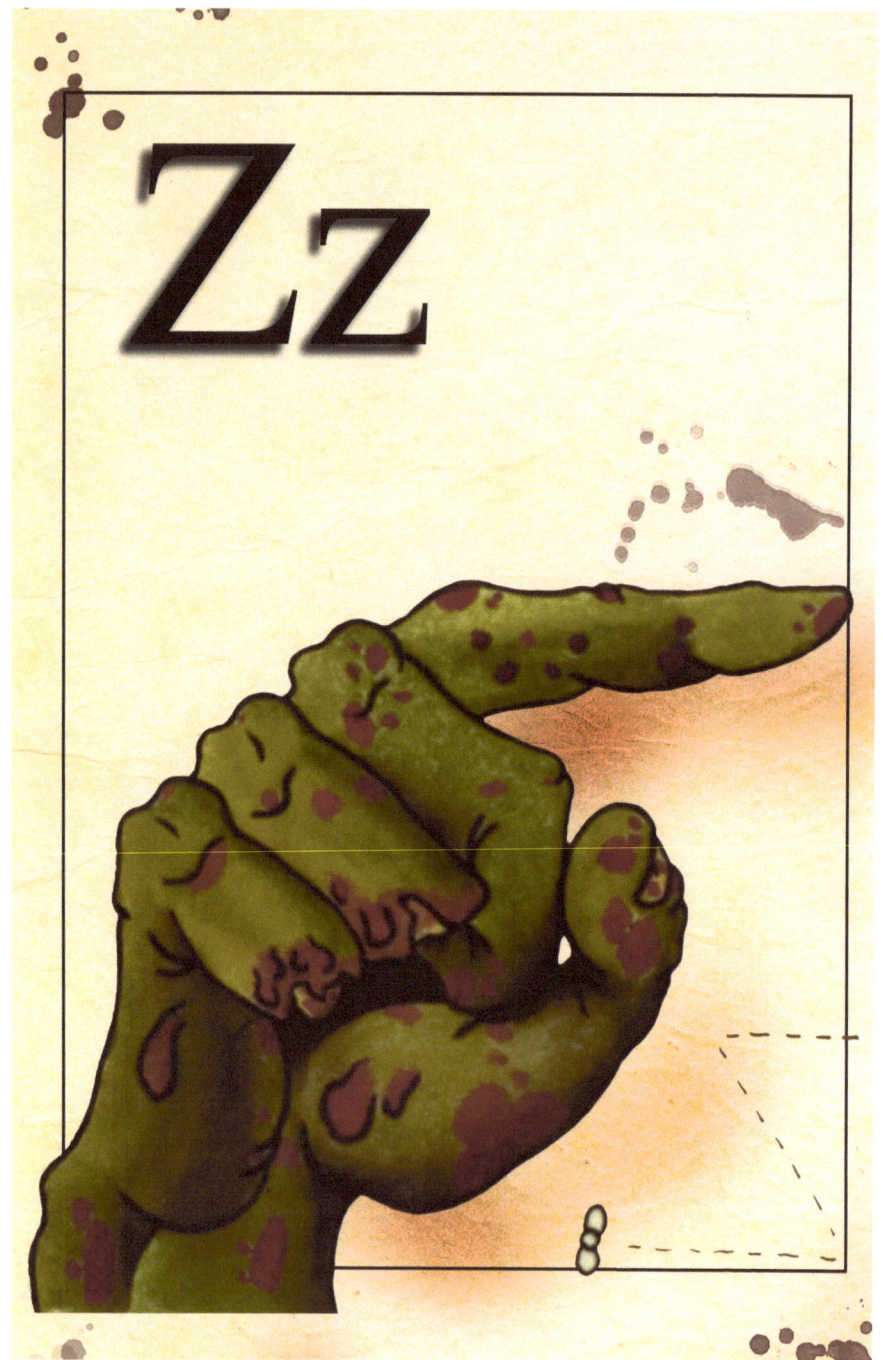

15 Spet 1976

I can smell it. Someone was careless in the r...
to evacuate. It started as with one, only one ...
ligent action. Someone was bitten and no one ...
noticed. How could they not notice? I guess the ...
will to survive outweighs any training provide...
the laboratory staff after all. They hid it f...
everyone for what I can only assume was a m...
of moments. It didn't take long, but by the t...
we discovered the infraction it was too late. T...
attacked another staff member and in the pan...
one of the cells was left unattended. The Zed
inside wasted no time, maybe it was the ...
movement. The noise. Most of the time they just
stand and stare, but as soon as it could, this
Zed attacked. Moving out into the fray, it tore
another staff member apart while they were ...
tracted by the initial attack. Why didn't they
just close off the room. The lives of those inside
weren't worth this. Now they are all over the
compound.

It seems that a bite from the infected travels through the body faster than the injection. The ones bitten have been turning within minutes. There is no way for us to control it, we've been overrun. Well I guess there is one way, the smell. The military is forcing an explosive chemical compound through our ventilation system. It won't be much longer before the facility self ignites. All of this research will have been for nothing. I just hope that someone reads this entry, finds our work here and understands that it is too dangerous. This virus must be destroyed, there is no controlling it. There is no taming the things that it creates. These zombies are nothing but killing machines. I thought they could be tamed, trained, taught to obey. I was wrong. If this virus isn't destroyed it will kill us all.

Notes:

1. National Institute on Deafness and Other Communication Disorders. http://www.nidcd.nih.gov/health/hearing/pages/asl.aspx

www.ingramcontent.com/pod-product-compliance
Lightning Source LLC
Chambersburg PA
CBHW040321220526
45473CB00009B/2525